PRACTICAL
FENG SHUI

Formulas for Success

LILLIAN TOO'S

PRACTICAL
FENG SHUI

Formulas for Success

ELEMENT

First published in Great Britain in 2000 by
ELEMENT BOOKS LIMITED
Shaftesbury, Dorset SP7 8BP

Published in the USA in 2000 by ELEMENT BOOKS INC.
160 North Washington Street,
Boston MA 02114

Published in Australia in 2000 by
ELEMENT BOOKS LIMITED
and distributed by
Penguin Australia Ltd
487 Maroondah Highway,
Ringwood, Victoria 3134

Designed and created for Element Books with
The Bridgewater Book Company Ltd

Element Books Limited
Editorial Director Sue Hook
Project Editor Kate Adams
Production Director Clare Armstrong
Text Editor Emma Callery

The Bridgewater Book Company
Art Director Terry Jeavons
Designer Alistair Plumb
Editorial Director Fiona Biggs
Project Editor Mark Truman
Photography Mike Hemsley, Walter Gardiner Photography
Illustrations Lorraine Harrison, Sarah Young, Rhian Nest James
Three-dimensional models Mark Jamieson
Picture research Liz Eddison

Printed and bound in Great Britain by
Butler & Tanner Ltd, Frome and London

ISBN 1 86204 563 1

For my dearest friend and Feng Shui mentor, Master Yap Cheng Hai,

with love and affection

CONTENTS

INTRODUCTION

The phenomenon of Feng Shui, an ancient practice of space enhancement, in these very modern times is due to the simple fact that it works. All over the world, people are developing a sensitivity to the energy flows within the environment; and excitedly learning how to harness this energy to bring success and happiness, great wealth, and good health into their lives. Feng Shui is about living in harmony with the energies of the earth. It is about tapping into the core of this energy to attract a good future and happiness. Two main approaches can be used to achieve good Feng Shui: one is by positioning one's home to balance its energy with physical structures in the environment – collectively known as Landscape Feng Shui; the other is by applying powerful formulas to offer optimum orientations that bring serious good fortune. This book is about the formulas and their practical applications.

Feng Shui

Feng Shui is the harnessing of wind and water to capture the dragon's vital cosmic breath or Chi – the force that circulates and moves in the environment, indoors and outdoors, in water, on land, across mountains and continents. Chi is everywhere. It is invisible, vibrating through the human body and throughout the world. This book contains classical formulas that encourage the flow of *Sheng Chi*, which brings good luck, and the dissolving of *Shar Chi*, which brings bad luck.

In spite of increasing worldwide popularity and a growing perception of its wonderful potential to bring good fortune, prosperity, and happiness, an aura of mysticism continues to surround the practice of Feng Shui. This has not stopped the ancient Chinese doctrine of space enhancement from finding acceptance in the consciousness of many people. Indeed, practitioners the world over have started successfully to penetrate the obscure domains of Chinese symbolism, divination, and astrology that comprise the spectrum of practices associated with Feng Shui. In the process, they are gaining an appreciation of our relationship with space, time, and the Universe.

Feng Shui is the science of living in harmony with the environment. It advises on whether to live in front of or behind mountains, in valleys or on high ground, in plains or on hillsides. Feng Shui recommends a way of siting homes to bring the greatest advantage, balance, and affluence to their owners. This comes from being at one with the natural landscapes, winds, and waters of the earth. Feng Shui holds out the covenant of a life of considerable bounty to those who follow its parameters and principles when arranging their homes.

WIND AND WATER

The two words *feng* and *shui* translate literally as *wind* and *water*. These two elements jointly express the power of nature's blowing and flowing aspects, and their manifestations affect the shapes and colors of surface landscapes. In turn, the fortune of homes and buildings built above, below, or around these landscapes are changed.

FENG SHUI ADVISES ON WHETHER TO LIVE IN FRONT OF OR BEHIND MOUNTAINS, IN VALLEYS OR ON HIGH GROUND, IN PLAINS OR ON HILLSIDES, IN ORDER TO ENJOY THE BENIGN INFLUENCE OF THE COSMIC CHI.

occurs and misfortune starts to happen. Losses are incurred. There is unhappiness. Failure rules the day. Sickness, tiredness, weariness, and pessimism become the pervasive mood. In these circumstances bad Feng Shui is often debilitating.

Feng Shui should not be viewed narrowly. It is neither just a science nor simply an art. Feng Shui is neither magic nor a religious practice, although there have been many instances when meditative visualizations, alternative remedial cures, and spiritual chanting of prayers have been known to powerfully enhance the practice of Feng Shui.

Feng Shui is a powerful complement to all the wonderful spiritual and alternative practices that have become so popular today. From the ayurvedic techniques that originate from India, to aromatherapy, to the practice of mental visualization, Feng Shui works its special brand of dragon magic. Nevertheless, for Feng Shui to bring added value to your life, it should be applied in consonance with the thinking person's common sense and rational judgment.

The theory offers guidelines for living in harmony with the winds and waters of the earth to bring about situations of great good fortune. The rationale is built on a broad-based body of doctrines, beliefs, symbolism, formulas, and application principles – all of which offer techniques for arranging spaces and places that successfully tap into good directions, locations, and orientations. When Feng Shui is correctly done and all the energies of a particular area are harmonious, the environment delivers happiness, prosperity, and abundant good luck. The mood is one of confidence, good will, and harmony. When Feng Shui is incorrectly applied, the opposite of good fortune

Do not rely on instinct and intuition alone. But yes, let them guide you. Do not let your overly imaginative mind attribute every piece of good fortune to Feng Shui – often, it merely sets a harmonious stage to allow great good fortune and prosperity to enter your life. So give yourself some credit as well.

By the same token, do not blame every piece of bad luck on Feng Shui. Your misfortunes and losses could be your own negative karma ripening – in which case Feng Shui can only help to alleviate any consequent suffering. Feng Shui does not have the power to overcome your karmic debts. It cannot dissolve misfortune if this is part of your destiny, but it does have the ability to improve bad times, reducing their severity to a bearable level. When your destiny and your Feng Shui work positively together, the results are often spectacular – Feng Shui can greatly enhance good periods of your life.

Feng Shui works only if it is practiced correctly, so it is vital to understand what you are doing. This is the bad news. The good news is that it is not difficult to get the methods of implementing Feng Shui correct. Although Formula Feng Shui requires a degree of exactness and objectivity, its use and application involve less subjectivity of judgment than other areas of Feng Shui, so it is much easier to practice.

THE ORIGINS OF FENG SHUI

The fountainhead of Feng Shui can be traced to the *I Ching* – the ancient classic *Book of Changes* on which almost the whole body of Feng Shui knowledge is based. Four great thinkers are associated with the *I Ching* – the founder Fu Hsi; King Wen; his son, the Duke of Chou; and Confucius, arguably the most

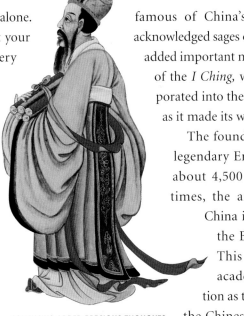

CONFUCIUS ADDED PRECIOUS THOUGHTS TO THE *I CHING*, THE ANCIENT CLASSIC *BOOK OF CHANGES*, ON WHICH ALMOST ALL FENG SHUI IS BASED.

famous of China's philosophers. Of these acknowledged sages of China, the last three each added important new thoughts to the wisdom of the *I Ching,* which, in turn, were incorporated into the development of Feng Shui as it made its way down the centuries.

The founder of the *I Ching* was the legendary Emperor Fu Hsi, who lived about 4,500 years ago. During those times, the ancient country that was China is said to have stretched to the Black Sea in western Asia. This probably fueled some academic debate and speculation as to the connections between the Chinese Fu Hsi and the Western Adam (from the Bible).

The *I Ching* that Fu Hsi founded is the source book of all Chinese thought and practice. It emphasizes crucial links between destiny and nature and offers insights into the Universe as a special something in which all things exist in an uninterrupted state of evolution. Fu Hsi is said to have looked upward to contemplate the images of heaven and looked downward to observe the patterns of earth, thereby gaining understanding of the laws of nature and of the influence of cosmic forces on the quality of all the life that resided below. In his wisdom, he founded a practice not unlike what we now know as Feng Shui. He taught his people how best to attune their homes to the moods and the rhythms of nature and thus provided them with a sense of harmonious living and security.

LANDSCAPE FENG SHUI

Although the origins of Feng Shui go back to antiquity (as far back as the ancient source book on which it is based), it has been formally practiced in China only since the Tang Dynasty (618–907 C.E.). Records from this period have survived the passage of time, and today provide invaluable clues to the special type of environmental Feng Shui practiced during that period of Imperial rule. Books detailing the principles of Landscape Feng Shui make up some of the major texts on which succeeding generations of practitioners based their knowledge.

Tang Dynasty Feng Shui emphasized the shape of the mountains and the direction of watercourses. A set of rules was developed that evolved around the celestial and mythical dragon. In describing the perfect Feng Shui formation, masters of that period incorporated three other celestial creatures into the metaphors – the White Tiger of the west to complement the Green Dragon of the east; the Red Phoenix of the south; and the Black Turtle of the north. Good Feng Shui was then lyrically expressed according to how mountain ranges, each representing the four celestial creatures, were supposed to be laid out in relation to each other. As a result, the Landscape Feng Shui techniques are based on shapes, contours, elevations, and the way in which all kinds of structures – both natural and artificial – are placed in relation to each other.

Good Feng Shui sites are said to require the presence of mountains, but more specifically this means undulating types of hill ranges. The presence of Green Dragon hills indicate there are White Tiger hills present too, which are also undulating – but for good Feng Shui they should be lower than the Green Dragon hills.

LANDSCAPE FENG SHUI TECHNIQUES ARE BASED ON SHAPES, CONTOURS, ELEVATIONS, AND THE WAY STRUCTURES – BOTH NATURAL AND ARTIFICIAL – ARE PLACED IN RELATION TO EACH OTHER.

COMPASS FORMULA FENG SHUI

No practitioner of Feng Shui can afford to be ignorant about the influence of shapes, forms, and elevations on the overall quality of Feng Shui. Indeed, Landscape Feng Shui is the most basic of Feng Shui theories and applications. However, emphasis on the physical lay of the land was soon deemed to be incomplete in the practice of Feng Shui, and eventually a second major system was developed, which collectively came to be known as Compass Formula Feng Shui.

This second system acknowledged the influence of metaphysical speculations and took a compass directional approach to the orientation of homes. Good and bad locations were expressed not only in dragon terms but also in accordance with specific compass directions. With the development and rise in popularity of Compass Formula Feng Shui, masters soon developed their own codes of practice, and the Luo Pan, or Feng Shui compass, became the repository of many Feng Shui masters' trade secrets. Formulas were jealously guarded and passed on only from master to favorite disciple near to the time of the master's death. Even when these formulas were passed on, there was no guarantee that the old master had not kept a vital last piece of information.

Compass Feng Shui formulations are based on the trigram symbols placed around the eight-sided Pa Kua in a specific arrangement. Formula Feng Shui also focuses on the significance of the numbers that are placed in the nine-sector Lo Shu magic square. In Feng Shui, the numbers 1 to 9 carry a multitude of meanings that range from extreme bad luck to the most auspicious good fortune. The ways in which they are arranged and the way they move (or "fly") around the grid and in the Chinese calendar make up the components of some very potent formulas, which are described in this book.

A COMING TOGETHER

In the late nineteenth and early twentieth centuries, the two schools of Feng Shui merged, and theories of each came to be seen as complementary. This combination became extremely popular in both Hong Kong and Taiwan, the two places outside China where the practice of Feng Shui flourished through the turn of the century. Today, modern practitioners in these two parts of the world customarily practice both of the schools, although the formulas preferred by masters in Taiwan differ from those in Hong Kong – both in method and in interpretation of the application of element Feng Shui.

Both countries have prospered and benefited from the extensive and pervasive influence of Feng Shui. While the practice was banned in China throughout most of the Mao Tze

THE COMPASS, FENG SHUI RULER, AND PA KUA ARE IMPORTANT TOOLS IN THE PRACTICE OF FORMULA FENG SHUI. THEIR FUNCTIONS AND CORRECT USE ARE DESCRIBED LATER IN THE BOOK.

Tung years, Feng Shui flourished in places outside China where migratory Chinese brought old customs and practices with them. Through the past hundred years, Feng Shui has gained increasing credibility from all sectors and social strata of society. Rich and poor alike embrace the advice of the Feng Shui masters with great reverence.

THE LUO PAN (TRADITIONAL FENG SHUI COMPASS) IS USED ONLY BY PROFESSIONALS.

By the 1950s, Feng Shui enthusiasts in Hong Kong, Taiwan, and Southeast Asia had added a third dimension to their Feng Shui practice. This was the application of symbolic Feng Shui. Conscious of the rich cultural heritage that lay behind their old customs and traditions, emigrant Chinese, homesick for their motherland, stretched deep into their own psyche and started to display what they regarded as good fortune symbols in their homes. Taiwan and Hong Kong Chinese began mass production of paintings, screens, urns, ceramics, cloisonné, and other representations of all the auspicious symbols to enable practitioners to supplement their practice of both Landscape and Compass Feng Shui with all the symbols of good fortune. The meanings and significance of these symbols of good fortune, some more popular than others, and some obscure and less well known, are all contained in the second in this series of Practical Feng Shui books. Symbolic Feng Shui works with great effectiveness when used in consonance with Formula Feng Shui.

THE HOUSEHOLD GODS — FUK (FAR LEFT), GOD OF WEALTH; LUK (CENTER), GOD OF HIGH RANK; AND SAU (LEFT), GOD OF LONGEVITIY — ARE TYPICAL SYMBOLS OF GOOD FORTUNE.

THE FORMULAS IN THIS BOOK

This book contains several of the most potent classical formulas of the Compass School of Feng Shui, of which the three most significant are the Eight Mansions Compass Formula, the Flying Star Formula, and the Water Dragon Formula. In addition, I have included three minor formulas that complement Feng Shui and can be incorporated for routine changes and fine-tuning. These formulas are no less important and are also less complex. Each formula has been thoroughly simplified. The complex portions of the formulations have been precalculated and summarized into useful work tables that are easy to refer to and to apply.

While each Compass Formula addresses different dimensions of the practice, they have all been incorporated into the Feng Shui Luo Pan, the traditional Feng Shui compass. The formulations are founded on the Pa Kua of the Later Heaven Arrangement of trigrams and on the Lo Shu square. The Eight Mansions direction and location recommendations are based on the theoretical underpinnings of Feng Shui interpretations as taught to Master Yap Cheng Hai by his master from Taiwan, a legendary figure in his own time.

SPATIAL FORMULAS

It is necessary to differentiate between formulas that address space concepts in Feng Shui and those that deal with time dimensions. Spatial formulas deal with directions and locations. These formulas offer the most auspicious orientations according to your lunar year of birth and your gender.

Once you are in possession of your auspicious compass directions, the practical uses are enormous. Indeed, if you did nothing but practice this one aspect of Formula Feng Shui you would be reasonably sure of enjoying excellent Feng Shui. Being in possession of the formula alone is, however, insufficient. You must also become adept at using the formula in its many different permutations. To do this effectively requires both experience and a good working knowledge of the main tools of Feng Shui.

Other spatial prescriptions address the fixed orientations of the home. This offers a framework for investigating whether a home is lucky or unlucky for different people based on their lunar calendar year of birth. Feng Shui formulas that deal with the arrangement of personal space must be practiced with an eye on the effect of forms and shapes – which comprise landscape considerations.

TIME DIMENSION FORMULAS

It is also necessary to take into consideration the effects of time dimension. The passage of time plays a vital part in Feng Shui. The most important formula of time dimension Feng Shui is Flying Star Feng Shui (also known as Sarn Yuan or Three Period Feng Shui – see pages 56–89)

THE SOUTHERN HEMISPHERE

All the recommendations in this book apply equally to countries in the Northern and Southern Hemispheres. Readers living in Australia, South America, and South Africa should take note of the fact that I have checked this point over and over again with several authentic and reliable Feng Shui masters who are well versed in the Compass Schools of Feng Shui. All of them agree that there is no difference in the applicability of formulations for the Northern or Southern Hemispheres.

This difference in interpretation has come about because of speculation that since the element of the south is fire this must refer only to the Northern Hemisphere where the source of warmth (fire) is the equator. The reason Feng Shui practitioners equate the south with fire is not the position of the equator, but because the trigram Li (which stands for fire) is placed south in the Later Heaven Arrangement of the trigrams around the Pa Kua (see page 27).

– a method of Feng Shui that is popular and widely practiced in Hong Kong. Flying Star Feng Shui uses numerology and the Lo Shu square almost exclusively in figuring out the effect of time on the various corners of any home or old building. This technique is said to represent the divinitive branch of Feng Shui practice.

Those who are adept at interpreting the meanings of the way the stars (or numbers) fly around the Lo Shu grid are able to forecast the good times and bad times of countries. Some have been known to be remarkably accurate when predicting the ups and downs of stock market and currency indices. In Hong Kong, a well-known investment bank – Credit Lyonnaise – commissioned what they named the Feng Shui index. This accurately tracked and predicted the movement of the Hang Seng stock market index for a couple years. It was eventually discontinued after lesser skilled masters took over the job and became less accurate in their predictions of the turning points of the market.

Time dimensions in Feng Shui are also based on the Lo Shu numbers of days, months, and years as contained in the Chinese calendar. Based on special formulations, it is possible to figure out the Feng Shui of timing of renovations, house moves, and starting dates for construction. These formulas, however, are complex and only a sampling of the more important annualized periods for undertaking renovations and constructions are given here as reference tables.

ASTROLOGICAL FORMULAS

Another popular method of Feng Shui widely used in Hong Kong is based on the astrological calculation of a person's year, month, date, and time of birth – collectively referred to as the Four Pillars or Eight Characters (*see* pages 104–115). The astrological formulas are less exact than other formulas and the prescriptions offered for good personalized Feng Shui depend on your skills in interpreting the excess or lack of the five elements – wood, fire, metal, earth, or water – in your life.

FENG SHUI FORMULAS CAN HELP DETERMINE THE BEST TIME TO REDECORATE OR RENOVATE YOUR HOUSE.

WATER FORMULAS

Finally, this book summarizes the prosperity Water Formulas, which are of special interest to those who have gardens. These formulas are said to be based on the *Water Dragon Classic*, famed for bringing great wealth to those fortunate enough to live in homes near natural Water Dragons. In the 1940s and 1950s, the formulas were formally recorded by one or two of the most learned Feng Shui masters of Taiwan. The secrets of water flows and exit directions were incorporated into the personal Luo Pans of these masters and only passed on to special disciples. One such disciple was Yap Cheng Hai who has generously allowed me to pass it on to the world through my books.

The Water Dragon Formula (*see* pages 116–133) deals with both water flows and moving bodies of water. Although based on separate and different formulas, they can be applied concurrently.

1

GETTING STARTED

Before delving deeper into the formulas that are provided in this book it is important to become acquainted with some basic information that is pertinent to much of what follows. In this chapter you will develop a knowledge of your home's basic characteristics and the direction in which it faces. You will also need to gather together some essential tools, and these are outlined on pages 20–21. The remainder of this chapter is concerned with explaining the Lo Shu grid and the Pa Kua. This information forms the core of many of the formulas, so understanding these basic tools will help you to become an excellent practitioner of Feng Shui.

Surveying Your Home

Always start a Feng Shui analysis with a preliminary physical survey of your home – both outside and inside. Assess the surrounding environment – the roads, hills, buildings, and neighbors' properties – to ensure that structures that are inadvertently hitting at the home are taken into account when applying the formulas on directions. Use the checklists below to survey first the exterior and then the interior of your home.

THE EXTERIOR

The exterior survey should take note of the following:

THE SHAPE OF THE WHOLE HOME

- Regular shapes are better than irregular ones. Irregular shapes lead to "missing corners" (*see* pages 24–25).
- Square shapes are of the earth element, and rectangular shapes are of the wood element. They are the easiest to work with in Compass Formula Feng Shui.
- L-shaped and U-shaped homes are inauspicious and more difficult to work with.

THE CONTOURS AND ELEVATIONS

- Is the back of the home higher than the front? If not, you will have to place a tall light at the back of the home before you start. It is vital that your main door does not face land that is higher than your home (directions are explained on pages 34–39).
- Is the left-hand side of your home (looking through your main door from the inside out) higher than the right-hand side of the home? If not, you need to place a tall light on the left-hand side of the home before you start.

THE NEIGHBORING BUILDINGS

- Are surrounding buildings higher than your home? If so, make sure the door you use as your main door is not facing any of these buildings.
- Is there a triangular-shaped roof from a neighboring building pointing directly at your main door? If so, you should reposition the door – try to use an auspicious direction (*see* pages 40–41).

THE SURROUNDING ROADS

- Is your home surrounded on all sides by roads? This is not a good configuration. Is it surrounded back and front by roads? This, too, is not good. Plant trees behind your house to simulate support.
- Is there a traffic circle in front of your home directly facing the main door? This is a good feature and you should try to tap the good energy.

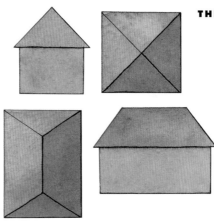

HOUSES IN REGULAR SHAPES ARE
GOOD IN FENG SHUI TERMS.

- Is there a straight road directly aimed at your main door? If so, move the door or use another one. When positioning a door for luck according to compass directions make sure it does not directly face an oncoming road. This is true of all the structures in your environment that are capable of sending harmful "poison arrows" toward you.

TOILETS, STOREROOMS, AND KITCHEN
- These are best placed in the inauspicious sections of your home, as explained later.

THE DEPTH AND WIDTH OF YOUR HOME
- Long houses tend to have long-lasting Feng Shui.

THE INTERIOR
The interior survey should note the following features:

THE SHAPE, SIZE, AND NUMBER OF ROOMS
- Regular shapes are again easier to work with. Try to regularize room shape with clever furniture layouts.

PLANT TREES BEHIND YOUR HOUSE TO SIMULATE THE SUPPORT OF THE BLACK TORTOISE.

DOORS AND WINDOWS
- Their position in the different rooms will establish the parameters of what you can and cannot do.

FURNITURE ARRANGEMENT
- In arranging furniture to tap into your auspicious directions, you must take account of other Feng Shui guidelines. For instance, in placing your bed to tap your best sleeping direction, you should not sleep with your head or feet pointed to the door.

Gathering the Tools

After your initial survey, gather together your tools. You will need a compass (a traditional Luo Pan or a modern Western compass) and a tape measure. You will also need to be familiar with the Lo Shu grid (*see* pages 24–25) and the Pa Kua (*see* pages 26–27). Then you can begin to explore the formulas.

COMPASSES

THE LUO PAN

In modern practical Feng Shui, the traditional Luo Pan compass is used only by professionals. Luo Pans usually contain the secret codes of different masters, so they are used only by those who have trained with the masters. However, a Western compass is a perfectly adequate alternative; you can apply the formulas here using it and the reference tables in this book.

The Luo Pan comprises concentric rings drawn around a magnetic compass. Its inner rings show the trigrams and orientations; the succeeding rings mark out the five elements with their Yin and Yang aspects, and the 24 directions that feature in most Compass Formulas of Feng Shui.

The directions reflect the detailed angles that must be observed when orienting doors and rooms as well as positions for sleeping, eating, and working. Each of the four cardinal and secondary directions are further subdivided into three directions, making a total of 24

directions (8 x 3 = 24). In Chinese Feng Shui parlance these are referred to as the 24 "mountains." In a traditional Luo Pan, the trigrams placed around the compass reflect both the Early Heaven as well as the Later Heaven Arrangements of the trigrams. The two arrangements separately define the Yin Pa Kua and the Yang Pa Kua, but the arrangement that concerns us here is the Later Heaven Arrangement (the Yang Pa Kua) because it determines the Feng Shui of all the abodes of the living (as opposed to homes of the dead) – *see* pages 26–27.

THE WESTERN COMPASS

Invest in a good Western magnetic compass. In Feng Shui, when we refer to the north we are referring to the magnetic north, which does not change wherever you are in the world, whether in the Northern or in the Southern Hemisphere.

Select a compass with directions marked out in degrees bearing north so that you are able to tell precisely which of the three subsections or "mountains" of a particular direction a door faces. Exact degrees of orientation are required when applying Flying Star Feng Shui and the Water Dragon Formula.

TAPE MEASURE

Dimensions need to be taken so that the home can be divided into nine separate sectors according to the nine-sector grid of the Lo Shu square, and it is important that they are accurate. These measurements determine where each corner of the home that corresponds to one of the eight primary and secondary directions starts and ends. The actual grid of your home doesn't have to be square, but each sector must be the same size.

In addition to a normal measuring tape, it is a good idea to invest in a Feng Shui ruler that marks out all the auspicious and inauspicious directions.

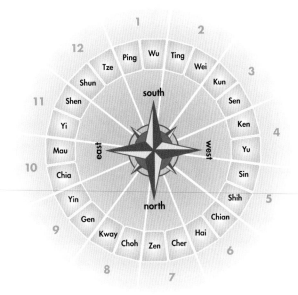

THE COMPASS ABOVE SHOWS THE CHINESE NAMES OF THE 24 MOUNTAINS. THESE ARE THE THREE SUB-SECTORS OF THE EIGHT DIRECTIONS OF THE COMPASS.

TOOLS OF THE TRADE: YOU WILL NEED A COMPASS (PREFERABLY MODERN) AND A TAPE MEASURE – THE TRADITIONAL FENG SHUI RULER IS A GOOD BUT NOT ESSENTIAL OPTION.

Taking Door Directions

The next step is to determine your bearings. The practice of Formula Feng Shui requires you to be very familiar with the compass directions of your home. If you live in an apartment, you should know the directions and bearing of your own apartment as well as those of the whole building in which your apartment is located. This means knowing the directions that both main doors face, because they each have a bearing on your Feng Shui.

Main door directions are always taken facing outwards. If your home has a yard with a path or a driveway you should take note of the direction and orientation of your whole home, and you must know the directions that both the gate and the main door face. In Feng Shui, the orientation of the main door is the single most important determinant of the type of energy that enters the home. If you get your main door oriented according to special Feng Shui formulas, this alone will bring you good fortune. The main door is the "kou" or mouth of the home, where the Chi enters. It is where misfortune is

DETERMINING THE EIGHT DIRECTION ZONES

In addition to taking directions at the main door, you should take directions from the center of the home in order to mark out the eight direction zones or corners of the home for applying the different formulas.

You should again take three readings, all from the same room. If the center of the home is located in a small room, the distance between the three readings can be reduced.

The difficulty faced by most practitioners is how to determine the center of the home if the shape of the home is irregular. It is often easier to estimate the location of the center from a layout plan after the dimensions have been accurately taken. Architectural or technical drawings of your home will make it easier to be accurate.

1 Take the first reading from just inside the door. Position the compass on the floor so that it is directly next to the door. What you are trying to determine is the direction your door faces, so turn the compass until the needle is aligned with north. Now you can determine the number of degrees bearing north that your main door faces. Note this down.

created if it is afflicted or hurt in any way by surrounding structures. In houses that have more than one entry door there is often confusion about which door is considered the main door. The classic texts describe the main door as the one most frequently used by residents to get in and out of the house.

Take three readings to determine the orientation and alignment of the main door (*see* below). In most cases, the three readings will yield slightly different results. As long as the difference in the three readings is less than 15 degrees, they are acceptable, and you should take an average of the three readings and deem this to be the direction your main door faces.

Where there is a large swing in the compass readings, it is advisable to take a look at spatial arrangements of furniture and electronic equipment. Large differences in compass readings often suggest an imbalance of energy, either because of the way the furniture has been arranged in the room or because the whole area itself is seismic, for instance in California or other places prone to earthquake activity. If this is so, you might want to invest in a more powerful surveyor's compass. Some Feng Shui masters would refuse to proceed until the compass readings have returned to normal. If the compass readings are inaccurate, the applications of the formula might be defective.

2 Take the second reading from 3 ft (1m) inside the main door, again with your compass placed on the floor. Use a Feng Shui ruler or a tape measure to determine the distance from the front door. Do not worry if the reading differs slightly from the first reading. Please note that you must always take directions from the inside looking out of the door.

3 Take the third reading 10–15 ft (3–5m) inside the door, once again making sure that your compass is placed straight on the floor. If the space inside your main door isn't this large, go to its center for this third reading.

The Lo Shu Grid

T he Lo Shu grid is important in understanding Feng Shui and, more specifically, is vital in the practice of Compass Formula Feng Shui. It contains a "magical" arrangement of numbers, eight of which relate to the cardinal and secondary compass points – and the central number relates to the center of the home. Superimposing the grid on a layout plan of your home is essential to the analysis of Feng Shui sectors.

HOW TO USE THE GRID

These are four simple steps in analyzing the Feng Shui of the various compass sectors of your home.

1 *If you do not have architectural or technical drawings of your home, draw your own site plan as accurately as possible.*

2 *Draw the Lo Shu grid on transparent paper and superimpose it on the plan, matching the orientation of the home with the sectors on the grid.*

3 *By superimposing the Lo Shu grid onto the layout plan, you will be able to identify afflicted corners, inauspicious sectors, and defective zones according to the formulas outlined in this book.*

4 *Carefully demarcate the grid sectors of your home and label them in accordance with the directions.*

Note: The space need not be a perfect square – the grid can be stretched horizontally or vertically to fit the layout. But each sector should be approximately the same size.

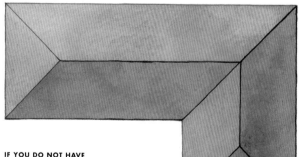

IF YOU DO NOT HAVE
ARCHITECTURAL OR TECHNICAL
DRAWINGS OF YOUR HOME, DRAW
YOUR OWN SITE PLAN (ABOVE).

THE LO SHU GRID (RIGHT) IS VITAL
IN THE PRACTICE OF FENG SHUI.
USE IT TO DEMARCATE THE
SECTORS OF YOUR HOME.

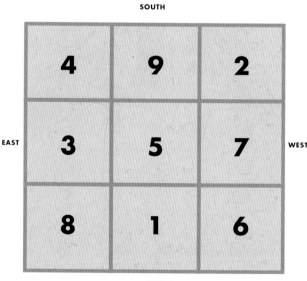

SOUTH

4	9	2
3	5	7
8	1	6

EAST · WEST

NORTH

THE VALUE OF THE GRID

Whatever the ground shape of your space, the Lo Shu grid offers you an instant starting point for undertaking your analysis and the application of Feng Shui formulas. Before you do this, memorize the numbers in the Lo Shu grid and their equivalent directions. In this way you will know which sector of the home is represented by which Lo Shu number.

Superimposing the Lo Shu grid over the layout enables you to:

- determine accurately the eight different sectors according to the compass directions,
- demarcate the center sector of the home,
- spot any missing or protruding corners,
- create a blueprint for your home for further Feng Shui analysis using both the spatial and time formulas.

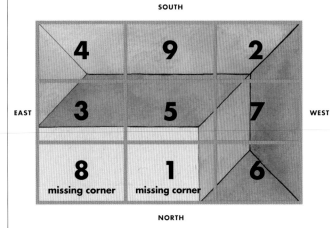

SUPERIMPOSING THE LO SHU GRID OVER THE LAYOUT OF YOUR HOME ENABLES YOU TO IDENTIFY YOUR "MISSING CORNERS" AND YOUR PROTRUDING CORNERS.

SUPERIMPOSING THE LO SHU GRID

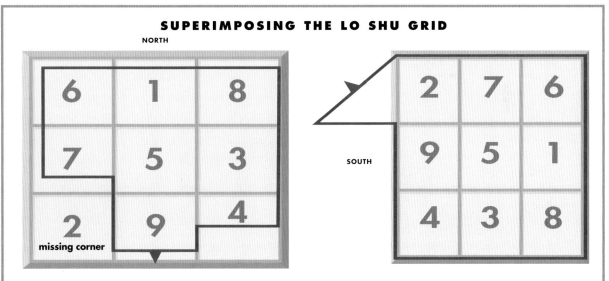

ABOVE: THE MAIN DOOR IS FACING SOUTH SO THE LO SHU GRID HAS BEEN TURNED AROUND TO MATCH. THE SOUTHWEST CORNER (2) IS MISSING. THIS MAY MEAN THE LUCK ATTRIBUTED TO THAT SECTOR (SEE PP 50–51) WILL BE MISSING. OVERCOME IT WITH AN EXTERNAL

LIGHT IN THAT AREA OR A MIRROR INSIDE ON THE ADJACENT WALL. THE SECOND EXAMPLE SHOWS THE MAIN DOOR FACING SOUTHWEST ON A PROTRUDING CORNER, WHICH EXACERBATES THE LUCK OF THE ADJACENT SECTOR (SOUTHWEST, 2).

Superimposing the Pa Kua

The Pa Kua was derived from the traditional source book – the *I Ching*. It is an eight-sided symbol that is used, among other things, to ascertain the trigram and element that relates to each direction already established by the Lo Shu grid. The trigrams are part of the *I Ching* and there are two Pa Kua arrangements that can be used when practicing Feng Shui: the Yin Pa Kua, or Early Heaven Arrangement, and the Yang Pa Kua, or the Later Heaven Arrangement. However, it is only this last that should be used inside the home. The Yin Pa Kua relates specifically to the houses of the dead – the Feng Shui of tombs.

Use the Pa Kua of the Later Heaven Arrangement, which places the trigrams Chien and Kun in the northwest and southwest respectively. Note the compass directions of each of the eight corners of your home and use them to determine the dominant or ruling element of each corner. In addition, each corner has other attributes that you can immediately determine, and these will be explored further in the chapter on the Nine Aspirations Formula on pages 48–55.

Armed with this knowledge you will be in an excellent position to start applying the different formulas. It is as easy as this. In later chapters, each of the formulas is examined in turn, indicating the various ways in which the different elements and attributes of each corner can be applied. This is in accordance with the different meanings of each corner as shown in the Pa Kua.

The Yin Yang symbol represented in the center of the Pa Kua reflects the way of heaven and earth. This implies that everything can be divided into the two mutually opposing and independent forces of Yin and Yang, following the belief that all things on earth consist of the unity of opposites. The symbols depicted within the eight sides of the Pa Kua and the corresponding trigrams reflect this dualistic view of the Universe.

DIFFERENT PRACTICES

Some Feng Shui practitioners have different methods for determining corners, and this may be confusing for those new to the practice of Feng Shui.

I have surveyed the literature on this particular Feng Shui formula and have noted that in the United States of America a very popular way of using this method is what I term the Fixed Pa Kua method, which does not use the compass. Instead, the eight aspirations are allocated to the corners of a home according to the position of the main door, and the main door is always taken to be the south. This means that as you walk into the home, the sector located directly opposite the main door is regarded as north. The actual compass direction is completely ignored.

However, I like to use a compass when applying this formula because I regard this method as being an offshoot of the Compass School. As such, I take my cue from the way all other Compass Feng Shui formulas are applied, especially those that use the Lo Shu square.

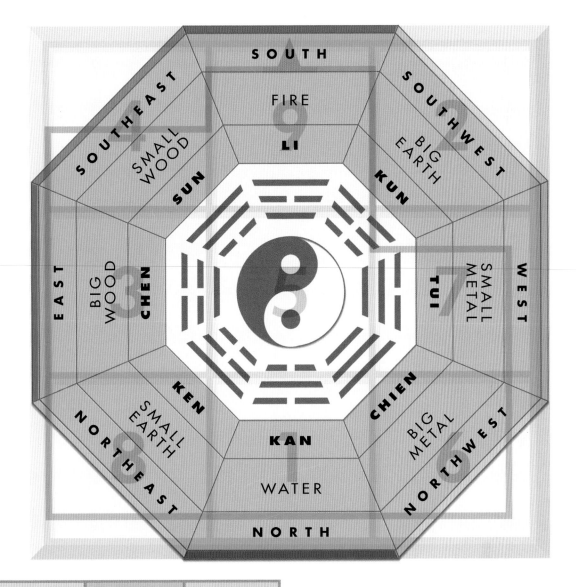

The Yang Pa Kua showing the Later Heaven arrangement with its directions, trigrams, elements, and numbers:

- SOUTH — FIRE — 9 — LI
- SOUTHWEST — BIG EARTH — 2 — KUN
- WEST — SMALL METAL — 7 — TUI
- NORTHWEST — BIG METAL — 6 — CHIEN
- NORTH — WATER — 1 — KAN
- NORTHEAST — SMALL EARTH — 8 — KEN
- EAST — BIG WOOD — 3 — CHEN
- SOUTHEAST — SMALL WOOD — 4 — SUN

Southeast	South	Southwest
Wood	Fire	Earth
East	Center	West
Wood	Earth	Metal
Northeast	North	Northwest
Earth	Water	Metal

EACH SECTOR OF THE HOME IS ASSOCIATED WITH ONE OF THE FIVE ELEMENTS; THE FORMULAS IN THIS BOOK SHOW HOW THIS KNOWLEDGE IS APPLIED TO BRING THE BEST FENG SHUI.

THE YANG PA KUA SHOWING THE LATER HEAVEN ARRANGEMENT IS SUPERIMPOSED ON THE LO SHU GRID AND HOUSE PLAN TO DETERMINE THE RULING ELEMENT IN EACH SECTOR OF YOUR HOUSE.

2

THE EIGHT MANSIONS FORMULA

The Eight Mansions (or Pa Kua Lo Shu) Feng Shui technique is a personalized method based on the year of birth and gender of the practitioner. Using a series of preformulated tables, which are presented in this chapter, you can determine auspicious and inauspicious directions and locations. This vital information will help you to orientate your home and your office in the most advantageous way, thus creating excellent Feng Shui. The Eight Mansions Formula has many applications – too numerous to cover in this book. However, if you study the practical applications suggested here, you will begin to get an idea of other ways of using the formula.

Kua Numbers

The Eight Mansions Formula is based on the lunar year of birth and on the gender of the person. These are the only two pieces of information that are required to discover your personal Kua number: *kua* means *sector*, as in Pa Kua (or eight sectors). The lunar year of birth is used because Feng Shui formulas are based on the lunar calendar but it is not necessary to have the entire horoscope requirements of hour, day, month, and year. The lunar year alone is sufficient.

In order to obtain your lunar year of birth, it is necessary to know your date of birth under the Western calendar. The Gregorian or Western calendar does not match the lunar calendar. In fact, the two systems are so different that the start of the lunar New Year varies from between late January to early February. Furthermore, in certain years, the lunar year has 13 instead of 12 months, and sometimes the lunar calendar records a year of double spring – what the Chinese refer to as a Lap Chun year – usually regarded as a good year.

To learn what your lunar year of birth is, check your birth date against the Chinese hundred-year calendar that is provided overleaf. If you were born before the Chinese New Year in any given year, then you need to subtract a year from your year of birth. However, if you are born after the Chinese New Year, then your lunar year of birth remains the same as your Western calendar year of birth.

The calendar is a summary reference table to make the Eight Mansions Formula really easy to remember and use. The table also gives you your Kua number, and once you know this you can proceed to the subsequent reference tables in this chapter for interpretation and applications.

FIGURING OUT A KUA NUMBER

All the Kua numbers are given in the hundred-year calendar overleaf, but it might be useful to know how these numbers are derived. Figuring out the Kua number requires a different formula for men and for women. This formula works for anyone born before the year 2000. After 2000, the formula changes, as outlined on the page opposite.

FOR MEN

Add the last two digits of your lunar year of birth. Keep adding the digits until you reduce it to a single number. Then subtract the single digit from 10 and the answer is your Kua number.

Example 1
If you were born on December 3, 1982: $8 + 2 = 10$ and then $1 + 0 = 1$ and then $10 - 1 = 9$, so your Kua is 9.

Example 2
If you were born on January 2, 1946, your lunar year was 1945 since you were born before the lunar new year. Thus: $4 + 5 = 9$ and then $10 - 9 = 1$, so your Kua is 1.

Example 3

If you were born on August 17, 1977: 7 + 7 = 14 and then 1 + 4 = 5 and then 10 − 5 = 5, so your Kua is 5.

FOR WOMEN

Add the last two digits of your lunar year of birth. Keep adding the digits until you reduce it to a single number. Add 5 to this number; the answer you end up with is your Kua number.

Example 1

If you were born on November 13, 1973:
7 + 3 = 10 and then 1 + 0 = 1 and then 5 + 1 = 6, so your Kua is 6.

Example 2

If you were born on January 2, 1933, your lunar year would be 1932 because you were born before the lunar new year. Thus: 3 + 2 = 5, then 5 + 5 = 10, and then 1 + 0 = 1, so your Kua is 1.

Example 3

If you were born on August 6, 1975: 7 + 5 = 12 and then 1 + 2 = 3 and then 5 + 3 = 8, so your Kua is 8.

BIRTH DATES AFTER 2000

For those born after the year 2000, the formula changes. I usually refer to this as the millennium bug in Feng Shui. Thus for boys who are born in the year 2000 and after, instead of deducting from 10, you should deduct from 9. For girls, instead of adding 5, you should add 6.

FOR BOYS

Example 1

If a boy is born on March 13, 2000: 9 − 0 = 9, so his Kua will be 9.

Example 2

If a boy is born on May 16, 2004: 9 − 4 = 5, so his Kua will be 5.

FOR GIRLS

Example 1

If a girl is born on September 4, 2003: 6 + 3 = 9, so her Kua will be 9.

Example 2

If a girl is born on July 25, 2006: 6 + 6 = 12 and then 1 + 2 = 3, so her Kua will be 3.

THE CHINESE HUNDRED-YEAR CALENDAR: 1912 TO 1960

WESTERN CALENDAR DATES	ANIMAL	MALE KUA	FEMALE KUA
18 February 1912 – 5 February 1913	Rat	7	8
6 February 1913 – 25 January 1914	Ox	6	9
26 January 1914 – 13 February 1915	Tiger	5	1
14 February 1915 – 2 February 1916	Rabbit	4	2
3 February 1916 – 22 January 1917	Dragon	3	3
23 January 1917 – 10 February 1918	Snake	2	4
11 February 1918 – 31 January 1919	Horse	1	5
1 February 1919 – 19 February 1920	Sheep	9	6
20 February 1920 – 7 February 1921	Monkey	8	7
8 February 1921 – 27 January 1922	Rooster	7	8
28 February 1922 – 15 February 1923	Dog	6	9
16 February 1923 – 4 February 1924	Boar	5	1
5 February 1924 – 23 January 1925	Rat	4	2
24 January 1925 – 12 February 1926	Ox	3	3
13 February 1926 – 1 February 1927	Tiger	2	4
2 February 1927 – 22 January 1928	Rabbit	1	5
23 January 1928 – 9 February 1929	Dragon	9	6
10 February 1929 – 29 January 1930	Snake	8	7
30 January 1930 – 16 February 1931	Horse	7	8
17 February 1931 – 5 February 1932	Sheep	6	9
6 February 1932 – 25 January 1933	Monkey	5	1
26 January 1933 – 13 February 1934	Rooster	4	2
14 February 1934 – 3 February 1935	Dog	3	3
4 February 1935 – 23 January 1936	Boar	2	4
24 January 1936 – 10 February 1937	Rat	1	5
11 February 1937 – 30 January 1938	Ox	9	6
31 January 1938 – 18 February 1939	Tiger	8	7
19 February 1939 – 7 February 1940	Rabbit	7	8
8 February 1940 – 26 January 1941	Dragon	6	9
27 January 1941 – 14 February 1942	Snake	5	1
15 February 1942 – 4 February 1943	Horse	4	2
5 February 1943 – 24 January 1944	Sheep	3	3
25 January 1944 – 12 February 1945	Monkey	2	4
13 February 1945 – 1 February 1946	Rooster	1	5
2 February 1946 – 21 January 1947	Dog	9	6
22 January 1947 – 9 February 1948	Boar	8	7
10 February 1948 – 28 January 1949	Rat	7	8
29 January 1949 – 16 February 1950	Ox	6	9
17 February 1950 – 5 February 1951	Tiger	5	1
6 February 1951 – 26 January 1952	Rabbit	4	2
27 January 1952 – 13 February 1953	Dragon	3	3
14 February 1953 – 2 February 1954	Snake	2	4
3 February 1954 – 23 January 1955	Horse	1	5
24 January 1955 – 11 February 1956	Sheep	9	6
12 February 1956 – 30 January 1957	Monkey	8	7
31 January 1957 – 17 February 1958	Rooster	7	8
18 February 1958 – 7 February 1959	Dog	6	9
8 February 1959 – 27 January 1960	Boar	5	1

WESTERN CALENDAR DATES	ANIMAL	MALE KUA	FEMALE KUA
28 January 1960 – 14 February 1961	Rat	4	2
15 February 1961 – 4 February 1962	Ox	3	3
5 February 1962 – 24 January 1963	Tiger	2	4
25 January 1963 – 12 February 1964	Rabbit	1	5
13 February 1964 – 1 February 1965	Dragon	9	6
2 February 1965 – 20 January 1966	Snake	8	7
21 January 1966 – 8 February 1967	Horse	7	8
9 February 1967 – 29 January 1968	Sheep	6	9
30 January 1968 – 16 February 1969	Monkey	5	1
17 February 1969 – 5 February 1970	Rooster	4	2
6 February 1970 – 26 January 1971	Dog	3	3
27 January 1971 – 14 February 1972	Boar	2	4
15 February 1972 – 2 February 1973	Rat	1	5
3 February 1973 – 22 January 1974	Ox	9	6
23 January 1974 – 10 February 1975	Tiger	8	7
11 February 1975 – 30 January 1976	Rabbit	7	8
31 January 1976 – 17 February 1977	Dragon	6	9
18 February 1977 – 6 February 1978	Snake	5	1
7 February 1978 – 27 January 1979	Horse	4	2
28 January 1979 – 15 February 1980	Sheep	3	3
16 February 1980 – 4 February 1981	Monkey	2	4
5 February 1981 – 24 January 1982	Rooster	1	5
25 January 1982 – 12 February 1983	Dog	9	6
13 February 1983 – 1 February 1984	Boar	8	7
2 February 1984 – 19 February 1985	Rat	7	8
20 February 1985 – 8 February 1986	Ox	6	9
9 February 1986 – 28 January 1987	Tiger	5	1
29 January 1987 – 16 February 1988	Rabbit	4	2
17 February 1988 – 5 February 1989	Dragon	3	3
6 February 1989 – 26 January 1990	Snake	2	4
27 January 1990 – 14 February 1991	Horse	1	5
15 February 1991 – 3 February 1992	Sheep	9	6
4 February 1992 – 22 January 1993	Monkey	8	7
23 January 1993 – 9 February 1994	Rooster	7	8
10 February 1994 – 30 January 1995	Dog	6	9
31 January 1995 – 18 February 1996	Boar	5	1
19 February 1996 – 6 February 1997	Rat	4	2
7 February 1997 – 27 January 1998	Ox	3	3
28 January 1998 – 15 February 1999	Tiger	2	4
16 February 1999 – 4 February 2000	Rabbit	1	5
5 February 2000 – 23 January 2001	Dragon	9	6
24 January 2001 – 11 February 2002	Snake	8	7
12 February 2002 – 31 January 2003	Horse	7	8
1 February 2003 – 21 January 2004	Sheep	6	9
22 January 2004 – 8 February 2005	Monkey	5	1
9 February 2005 – 28 January 2006	Rooster	4	2
29 January 2006 – 17 February 2007	Dog	3	3
18 February 2007 – 6 February 2008	Boar	2	4

East and West Groups

Now that you have your Kua number you can determine the directions that are auspicious and inauspicious for you. According to the Eight Mansions Formula, every person in the Universe is born with four auspicious directions and four inauspicious directions. To establish your own set of directions you first need to establish whether you are an East Group or West Group person, which is directly related to your Kua number, previously ascertained.

Your auspicious and inauspicious directions depend on whether you are an East Group person or a West Group person. To find out whether you are an East or a West Group person, refer to the table on the opposite page.

East Group people will have great good fortune by orientating their Feng Shui toward the East Group directions. They should avoid any of the West Group directions since these are deemed to be extremely unlucky for East Group people.

Similarly, West Group people will enjoy excellent Feng Shui if they orientate their homes and personal spaces to tap into the West Group directions. They must try at all costs to avoid the East Group directions since these will spell misfortune for them.

EAST AND WEST HOMES

One of the most significant and potent ways of tapping into excellent direction luck according to this formula is to orientate your main door so that it faces one of your four auspicious directions. In the reference tables later in this chapter, you will find that, based on your Kua number, each of the four auspicious directions is further finetuned. The success, health, romance, and personal development for every person differs according to his or her Kua number.

Most of us would naturally want to orientate our homes to tap the best success luck, but before doing this it is important to be aware of the important guidelines that determine east and west homes.

The classic text on this formula says that, "A person who belongs to the East Group should live in an east home, while a person who belongs to the West Group

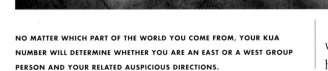

NO MATTER WHICH PART OF THE WORLD YOU COME FROM, YOUR KUA NUMBER WILL DETERMINE WHETHER YOU ARE AN EAST OR A WEST GROUP PERSON AND YOUR RELATED AUSPICIOUS DIRECTIONS.

should reside in a west home. A home is defined as being east or west based on where it is sitting. The sitting position is in turn determined according to the direction the main door is facing, being the opposite."

Thus when the main door faces east, the home is said to be a west home since west is the opposite of east: the home sits in the opposite direction to where its main door faces. Since west is a West Group direction, the home is said to be a west home. Thus if you belong to the East Group and your best direction happens to be east, simply by orientating your main door to face east, you would have inadvertently made it a west home. In other words, by orientating to face your best direction you have ended up staying in a home that brings bad luck to you!

I remember agonizing over this point with Master Yap when we first studied the formula directly from the old texts. It was not until much later when we had come to the end of the book that the explanation was forthcoming through indirect case examples cited.

So, if you are an East Group person, you should orientate your main door to face either north or south since the opposite direction of these two directions are both East Group. If either of these two directions happens to be your most auspicious success direction, then you are said to have the luck to tap your best direction. If you are a West Group person, you should orientate your main door to face either southwest or northeast for the same reasons.

Thus East Group people whose Kua numbers are 1 and 9 and West Group people whose Kua numbers are 6 and 7 cannot use their best success directions for the main door. Having clarified this important matter, we can now proceed to look at the auspicious and inauspicious directions in detail.

ORIENTING THE MAIN DOOR OF YOUR HOME TO FACE ONE OF YOUR BEST SUCCESS DIRECTIONS WILL CREATE AUSPICIOUS FENG SHUI.

EAST AND WEST GROUP PEOPLE

YOUR KUA NUMBER	EAST OR WEST GROUP
1	East
2	West
3	East
4	East
5	West
6	West
7	West
8	West
9	East

The East Group directions are east, southeast, north and south. The West Group directions are west, southwest, northwest, and northeast.

Auspicious Directions and Locations

First look at your auspicious directions, each of which attracts a slightly different kind of good luck. The auspicious directions for each individual shown in the table opposite apply equally to directions and locations. It is important to make a clear distinction between direction and location. When you apply the formula, you will find it may not always be possible to tap the direction and location you want – often it is a choice between one or the other.

In Feng Shui it is impossible to get everything correct. But as long as you are able to implement about 70% of good Feng Shui recommendations, you should be reasonably assured of enjoying good fortune.

• **Direction:** the direction you are facing, or your door is facing, or your head is pointing to. This is important when you are sleeping, sitting, or working.

• **Location:** a specific sector of the home corresponding to a specific direction – superimpose the Lo Shu grid on your house plan to determine these. This helps identify lucky or unlucky locations or sectors in the home.

1 THE SHENG CHI DIRECTION

This is the name given to your most auspicious direction – it is translated as "generating breath." This is the direction that you should face when working, negotiating, or giving an important presentation since it brings enormous success luck. It is also the direction your head should be pointing when you are sleeping. The sheng chi location and direction

is what you need to focus on if money and career luck are what you are looking for. If it is difficult to orientate facing your sheng chi direction, you should try to sit, work, sleep, or eat in your sheng chi location.

In any office, try to select your space according to your sheng chi location. You should also always endeavor to sit facing your sheng chi direction. At home it is excellent if your main door is facing your sheng chi direction, or if it is located in the sector that corresponds to the sheng chi. It is also excellent to sleep in the corner that represents your sheng chi. But please remember that most people cannot tap their sheng chi all the way.

LOCATION REFERS TO A SPECIFIC SECTOR IN YOUR HOME, WHILE DIRECTION REFERS TO WHERE YOU ARE FACING OR WHERE YOUR HEAD IS POINTING WHEN YOU SLEEP.

NORTH

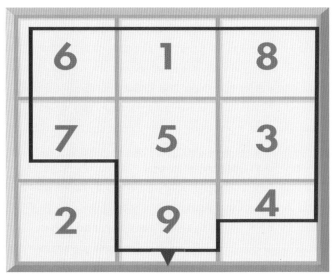

THE FOUR AUSPICIOUS DIRECTIONS/LOCATIONS

KUA NUMBER	SHENG CHI	TIEN YI	NIEN YEN	FU WEI
1	southeast	east	south	north
2	northeast	west	northwest	southwest
3	south	north	southeast	east
4	north	south	east	southeast
5 male	northeast	west	northwest	southwest
5 female	southwest	northwest	west	northeast
6	west	northeast	southwest	northwest
7	northwest	southwest	northeast	west
8	southwest	northwest	west	northeast
9	east	southeast	north	south

2 THE TIEN YI DIRECTION

This translates as "doctor from heaven" and symbolizes good health and longevity. It is considered to be the second best direction for wealth, but is exceptionally potent in curing anyone who may be suffering from prolonged and inexplicable illnesses. If poor health is your problem, you should tap your tien yi direction. The best way to do this is to use your oven or kettle so that the food you eat or the water you drink is cooked or boiled with energy coming from your tien yi direction.

3 THE NIEN YEN DIRECTION

This translates roughly as "longevity with many descendants;" it brings wonderful family, marriage, relationship, and descendants luck. Those who have problems getting married, in their marriage, or conceiving should activate their nien yen direction. This is how my husband and I succeeded in starting a family after ten years of a childless marriage. If your children are giving you a hard time, you can change their bed directions so that their heads point to their nien yen directions. They will be more family oriented and obedient!

4 THE FU WEI DIRECTION

Fu wei offers excellent education and personal development luck. Some masters also refer to this as the "wisdom" direction. If the main door of the home faces the fu wei direction of the younger members of the household, especially if they are at college or university, they will benefit from enormous luck that is manifested in excellent exam results and recognition. Schoolchildren and students should sit at their desks facing their respective fu wei direction.

WATCHPOINT

Orientate your rice cooker so that the source of energy that is cooking the food is coming from your tien yi direction.

Inauspicious Directions and Locations

Equally important as knowing what are your auspicious directions is knowing the relative severity of each of the four bad luck directions. Bad luck can mean accidents and mishaps, troublesome people, grievous harm to family and business, or even death. These directions are shown in the table below.

1 THE HO HAI DIRECTION

This is the least harmful of the four directions/locations. Translated literally it refers to accidents and mishaps. Ho hai leads to disasters that can be salvaged, and the misfortune rarely spells the end of everything. Thus if you are sleeping with your head pointed to your ho hai direction, you could well meet with an accident, or get sick, or be blamed for something that goes wrong.

2 THE WU KUEI DIRECTION

This is translated as the five ghosts direction. It is the second worst of the four bad directions, and it brings troublesome people who cause you problems, such as employees who work against you, friends who betray you, and family members who cause you worry. In severe cases, this direction brings misfortune to the youngest children in the household.

If the main door of the home is facing the wu kuei direction of the family patriarch, there will be many quarrels and a lot of negative noise in the home. There can be no peace.

On the other hand, this is an excellent direction to tap for locating the kitchen, since the stove is very powerful in pressing down the bad luck of the "five ghosts" of wu kei.

THE FOUR INAUSPICIOUS DIRECTIONS/LOCATIONS

KUA NUMBER	HO HAI	WU KUEI	LUI SHA	CHUEH MING
1	west	northeast	northwest	southwest
2	east	southeast	south	north
3	southwest	northwest	northeast	west
4	northwest	southwest	west	northeast
5 male	east	southeast	south	north
5 female	south	north	east	southeast
6	southeast	east	north	south
7	north	south	southeast	east
8	south	north	east	southeast
9	northeast	west	southwest	northwest

3 THE LUI SHA DIRECTION

This is a more serious direction since these two words literally mean the six killings. This is the direction that spells grievous harm to family and business. There will be financial loss and there could even be death. Six types of misfortune will befall anyone who sleeps with their head pointed to the lui sha direction or has the main door facing this direction. However, it is an excellent idea to locate toilets and kitchens in the lui sha location since this will effectively press down on misfortune caused by the bad luck direction.

4 THE CHUEH MING DIRECTION

This is the worst of the four bad directions. It means the total loss of everything and in certain circumstances

IF YOU SLEEP WITH YOUR HEAD POINTED TO YOUR HO HAI OR INAUSPICIOUS DIRECTION, YOU COULD MEET WITH AN ACCIDENT, OR GET SICK, OR BE BLAMED FOR SOMETHING THAT GOES WRONG.

this direction can also spell the death of the entire family. Total loss means just that – all the children wiped out, no descendants, and a destruction of the family name. When the main door of the home faces the chueh ming direction and the sleeping or sitting directions are pointed to the chueh ming, the misfortune experienced is exceedingly difficult to bear. This direction and location must be avoided at all costs since it can be fatal. The only time this direction's bad luck is overcome is during periods when the Flying Stars are favorable.

Applying the Formula

Now that you possess your good and bad directions, there are several ways in which you can immediately activate your orientations. There is no need to select an auspicious day to make these changes. It is important only to observe the main taboo of not moving furniture around during the night. The best time to make Feng Shui changes is always during the morning when the sun is out. The presence of Yang energy lends extra potency to the changes.

MAIN DOOR DIRECTIONS

The main door of your home or office is the most important thing to attend to. The main door should ideally face your best, i.e., your sheng chi, direction (*see* the table opposite). If you cannot do this then you simply must choose one of the other auspicious directions. Above all else, though, you should make certain

that the door is not facing your chueh ming, or total loss, direction.

If husband and wife have diametrically opposite directions, the conventional wisdom is to go with the direction of the man of the home or the breadwinner. In my own home I have two doors – one to accommodate my husband's direction and one to accommodate mine. This has worked brilliantly for us for about twenty years now.

In applying the formula to the main door orientation do remember the east and west home constraints on the use of the East and West Group directions (*see* pages 34–35). If you are an East Group person only those with Kua numbers 3 or 4 may use their sheng chi direction, which is south or north, since both these directions belong to the East Group.

Similarly among West Group people, only those with Kua numbers 2, 5, and 8 are able to use their best direction for the main door. Northeast and southwest are directly opposite each other so they can face a West Group direction and still be deemed to be staying in a west home.

THE MOST BENEFICIAL DIRECTION FOR A BEDROOM DOOR TO FACE IS THE NIEN YEN DIRECTION, WHICH IS BENEFICIAL FOR FAMILY HARMONY, ESPECIALLY BETWEEN SPOUSES.

WHAT MAIN DOOR DIRECTIONS MEAN

IF YOUR KUA NUMBER IS	AND YOUR MAIN DOOR IS FACING
1	south, your cupboard is full of food and money.
	east or southeast, there are many descendants.
2	northwest, husband and wife will be harmonious.
	northeast or west, you will get honor from the king.
3	southeast, you will gain promotion and have many good children.
	south or north, you will get fame and riches.
4	east, your family will have brilliant scholars.
	south or north, your prosperity will last.
5 male	same as 2, above.
5 female	same as 8, below.
6	southwest, you will be rich and prosperous.
	northeast or west, you and your descendants will be extremely prosperous and wealthy.
7	northeast, your family will be prosperous.
	northwest or southwest, your ancestors' property will grow and expand under your care.
8	west, you will have many descendants.
	northwest or southwest, your home will be filled with wealth, prosperity, and gold.
9	north, you will have plenty of gold and silver in the family.
	east or southeast, you will have intelligent sons.

OTHER DOOR DIRECTIONS

The orientation of other doors within the home or office can be fixed according to the auspicious directions of the occupant of the room. Thus sons and daughters can calculate their own directions and select bedrooms that benefit them. However, remember that the most beneficial direction for a bedroom door to face is the nien yen direction (the third auspicious direction), which is beneficial for family harmony, especially between spouses. It is not necessary to tap the sheng chi direction for everything, but it is important to face one of your four good directions. If this is not possible, then the bedroom should be located in the sector of the home that represents one of your four good locations.

The bedroom door should also not be afflicted with any of the various door taboos. For instance, it should not face a sharp edge, a corner, a staircase, or a toilet.

> ### WATCHPOINT
>
> **The bedroom door should not be afflicted with any of the door taboos – it should not face a sharp edge, a staircase, a corner or a toilet.**

AUSPICIOUS DIRECTIONS AT WORK

Your sitting position at work should be facing one of your four auspicious directions and, if possible, the sheng chi direction. If you do nothing else but use this one single tip, you will find your career luck really taking off. You will meet with success with less effort and all your hard work will pay off in terms of recognition, promotion, and more money. Your mind will be clear and the decisions you make will lead you to prosper and advance in your career.

If you are in business, facing your sheng chi direction allows excellent prosperity luck to come to you. When moving the desk to accommodate your most favorable sitting direction, always observe all the taboos of Feng Shui – the main one of which is that you should not sit with your back to the door. If you can, position your desk diagonal to the door and face your sheng chi direction. The result will be excellent success in your career.

An office is not the same as the home. In the office, colleagues, employees, and bosses interact with you. They are not family so you should protect yourself against betrayal. Also avoid having your back to the window unless there is a building outside that acts as back support. When arranging your office situation always be aware of poison arrows, sharp angles, and overhead beams. Avoid them at all costs.

Face your best direction when negotiating, sitting in a boardroom, making a presentation, being interviewed or making a speech. To tap into your best direction continuously, you have to memorize your four auspicious directions. It is a good idea to carry a pocket compass wherever you go. Make it a habit to check your orientations quickly whenever you have an important meeting or presentation. After a while it will grow into a routine. I have been checking my directions in this way for well over twenty years. When you are negotiating, it is particularly useful to sit facing your best direction.

When you travel on business or go to an important meeting, you should always endeavor to travel from one

MARGINS OF ERROR

When aligning doors, sitting, and sleeping positions, the margin of error can be around two degrees. In areas where compass readings can be unreliable (due to seismic activity underground) this formula can tolerate a slightly higher margin of error.

of your four auspicious directions. For instance, if you are a West Group person, then traveling from New York to London will mean you are traveling from the west and this will be auspicious. If you have to also be in Hong Kong it is better to go via London. This is because if you go via the Pacific you would be traveling from the east and that would not be good Feng Shui. If the actual direction is from the northeast however, it will be fine since the northeast is also a West Group direction. Make this quick analysis each time you plan a business trip and select the route that brings you the most luck.

When you relocate to another country or move home you should also travel or move from one of your four auspicious directions, and preferably from your sheng chi direction if it is a career-related or business relocation that you are making.

SLEEPING DIRECTIONS

The sleeping orientation should have your head pointing toward one of your four auspicious directions. This ensures that as you sleep your own Chi is recharged with energy that comes from your most auspicious direction. If you can align the bed in such a way as to tap your best direction and if the door into the bedroom is also facing an auspicious direction, then your bedroom will be a source of excellent good fortune. The sleeping direction is so important that even if you have to position the bed at a slightly awkward angle to the rest of the room it is still a good idea to do so. But do observe the major taboos of bed location. Make sure the bed is not directly facing the door. Nor should it be placed between the entrance door and the toilet door. Most important, do not let the bed stand in the middle of the room without back support.

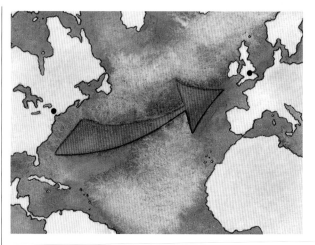

WHEN YOU PLAN A BUSINESS TRIP, SELECT THE ROUTE THAT WILL BRING YOU MOST LUCK.

STOVE AND KITCHEN DIRECTIONS

According to the old books on the Eight Mansions Formula, this application is one of the most potent applications of all. The fire mouth of your stove or oven should face one of your auspicious directions and most preferably face the tien yi direction (*see* pages 36–37). It should not face one of the four inauspicious directions. The fire mouth is defined as the source of energy for cooking your food. With electric stoves, ovens, and kettles, the fire mouth is where the electrical plug joins the appliance.

In households that use gas the fire mouth is often difficult to locate and the easiest way of meeting this Feng Shui requirement is to use a rice cooker or kettle to represent the cooking utensil. For a kettle or electric stove, it is the direction that the socket faces as it goes into the implement. For a gas stove, the fire mouth is defined as the direction the mouth faces because this is where the gas enters the stove.

WATCHPOINT

When arranging your office always look out for poison arrows – sharp angles and overhead beams. Avoid them at all costs.

Using Auspicious Lo Shu Locations

Activating your auspicious directions is the most obvious way of using the Eight Mansions Formula, but you can also benefit from being in one of your auspicious locations – these correspond to your lucky directions. Superimpose the nine-sector Lo Shu grid onto a layout plan of your home, room, or office to identify your lucky locations.

BEDROOM LOCATIONS

Each occupant of the home should ideally be located in the sector that corresponds to one of his or her auspicious directions. Auspicious energy is then enhanced by each person aligning his or her head to point in the sheng chi direction. Furthermore, if the door into the bedroom also faces the occupant's sheng chi direction, powerful Feng Shui will have been activated. This provides the perfect bedroom orientation and alignment.

Getting all three of these applications is usually difficult. Satisfying two out of three can be easier and is good enough. In fact, just being able to orientate your head correctly is excellent. It is seldom practical for everyone in a household to get everything perfect from a Feng Shui perspective, but as long as the important orientations are arranged correctly, i.e. according to the four auspicious directions, the Feng Shui is generally regarded as having been taken care of.

TOILET AND KITCHEN LOCATIONS

Feng Shui considers toilets and kitchens to have negative influences because they are used for washing and cleaning, and the garbage of the household accumulates there before being thrown away. These rooms

IN THIS BEDROOM, THE OCCUPANT'S KUA IS 4. FROM THE REFERENCE TABLES ON PAGES 36–37 YOU WILL SEE THAT HIS SHENG CHI DIRECTION IS NORTH, WHICH CORRESPONDS TO THE LO SHU SECTOR 1. HIS BEDROOM AND SLEEPING POSITION ARE ALIGNED PERFECTLY, SO HE WILL BENEFIT FROM EXCELLENT FENG SHUI.

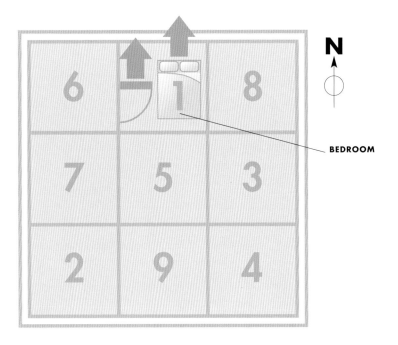

N

BEDROOM

KITCHEN AND OVEN ORIENTATIONS

IF THE KITCHEN OR OVEN IS IN:	THIS WILL BE THE RESULT:
Sheng chi location	Miscarriage, unpopularity, no livelihood.
Tien yi location	Will get sick, difficulty in recovery.
Nien yen location	No marriage opportunity, lots of quarrels and misunderstandings.
Fu wei location	No money, no longevity, and always short of money.
Chueh ming location	Lots of sons, money, servants, good health.
Lui sha location	Family very steady, no disaster, no fire.
Ho hai location	Will not lose money, no illness.
Wu kuei location	No fire, no robbery, no sickness, success.

should therefore be located where possible in those parts of your home that represent your four inauspicious directions. In addition, toilets and kitchens are believed to be able to press down on bad luck and consequently to control any Shar Chi (inauspicious energy) or excessively Yin energy that may be present in those sectors of the home. Toilets are preferably located in the chueh ming (total loss) sector or in one of the other unlucky sectors. This may be a difficult guideline to follow if other occupants of the household have

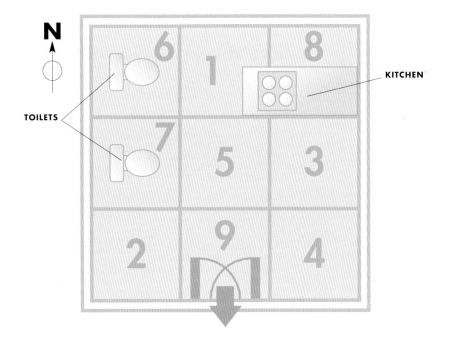

THIS EXAMPLE SHOWS WHERE THE KITCHEN AND TOILETS OF A PERSON WITH KUA NUMBER 3 CAN BE LOCATED. THIS APPLIES EQUALLY TO BOTH MALES AND FEMALES. THE INAUSPICIOUS DIRECTIONS OF A PERSON WITH KUA NUMBER 3 (FROM LEAST BAD TO WORST) ARE SOUTHWEST (HO HAI, 2), NORTHWEST (WU KUEI, 6), NORTHEAST (LUI SHA, 8), AND WEST (CHUEH MING, 7). THUS A TOILET IS LOCATED IN THE WEST, THE KITCHEN IS LOCATED IN 8 (WHICH IS THE NORTHEAST), AND THE BATHROOM IS LOCATED IN 6 (THE NORTHWEST). IT IS NEVER A GOOD IDEA TO HAVE TOILETS OCCUPY A LARGE SPACE. THE BEST ARRANGEMENT IS FOR THE TOILET TO OCCUPY ONLY A SMALL PART OF ANY COMPASS SECTOR.

THE EXAMPLE SHOWN HERE IS THE LAYOUT OF
A SALES OFFICE. THE LO SHU SQUARE HAS BEEN
SUPERIMPOSED ONTO THE OFFICE LAYOUT. GEORGE,
ONE OF THE SALES EXECUTIVES, HAS A KUA NUMBER
OF 6 AND HIS ROOM IS LOCATED IN SECTOR 3 (EAST),
WHICH IS INAUSPICIOUS FOR HIM. BUT HE IS FACING
WEST, WHICH IS HIS BEST DIRECTION. IF HE CAN
CHANGE TO THE ROOM IN SECTOR 7 (WEST) AND SIT
FACING NORTHEAST IT WILL BE BETTER – OR IF HE
CAN CHANGE TO THE ROOM IN SECTOR 8
(NORTHEAST) AND SIT FACING WEST HIS SALES
CAREER WILL IMPROVE HANDSOMELY. SALES OFFICES
SHOULD ALLOCATE ROOMS TO THEIR SALES FORCE
ACCORDING TO THEIR BIRTH DATES TO ENSURE EACH
PERSON ENJOYS PERSONALIZED CAREER LUCK. THE
COMPANY IS SURE TO BENEFIT.

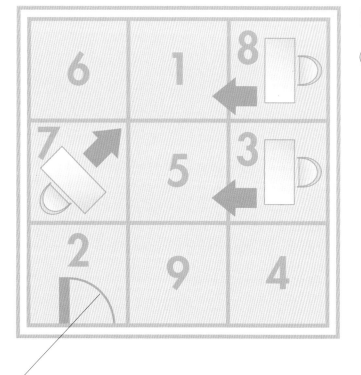

ENTRANCE TO OFFICE

different Kua numbers and therefore different inauspicious directions. In such cases, it is advisable to plan the Feng Shui according to the patriarch or breadwinner's Kua number and directions because it is especially important that toilets and kitchens are not placed in the patriarch's sheng chi location.

Kitchens should also be located in the inauspicious sectors. However, the fire mouth of the rice cooker or oven must be made to face an auspicious direction (*see* page 43 and table on previous page).

As bad luck is being "burned away" in the unlucky site, the fire mouth (the source of energy generally used to cook the food for the family) will be efficiently bringing in good luck from the auspicious direction.

OFFICE AND DESK LOCATIONS

In addition to facing an auspicious direction, the exact location of your office desk has direct relevance to the quality of your Feng Shui luck at work. Thus, Eight Mansions Feng Shui always advises that your desk or private office should be located in that part of the office or building that represents your sheng chi corner. If this is not possible at least try to locate it in one of the other three auspicious locations. Any one of the inauspicious sectors spells varying degrees of bad luck. Once you are located in a favorable corner you can then also arrange the desk so that your sitting direction is facing your best or at least one of your good directions.

FINAL ADVICE ON EIGHT MANSIONS FENG SHUI

The principles behind the reference tables on Eight Mansions Feng Shui are extremely potent and will definitely improve your Feng Shui if implemented correctly. The interpretation of formulas is not difficult, but combining theory, wisdom, and ideology to the practical reality of everyday living can often be challenging. Usually the multiplicity of "things to check" can be rather overwhelming, and the whole exercise can be tiresome. Much patience is required. But the results are often so good that I urge you to hang in there and stay with it.

The theory of Feng Shui is not difficult. Even the cultural complexities associated with the premier symbols are not beyond most of us. Doctrines and ideologies, however, are one thing. Practice and efficacy are something else. In the final analysis, how well and fast Feng Shui works at improving or enhancing your luck should be the criteria.

I am mindful of the difficulties of applying Feng Shui formulas at the practical level, having experienced the frustration of not knowing exactly what to do. My advice is to try to apply the formula to your particular situation and get some additional practice by helping others. With experience often comes insight. You will progressively become better and better at it until the Eight Mansions Formula becomes so easy you can practice it for yourself effortlessly. Carry a compass with you wherever you go. By simply facing your auspicious directions in all your encounters with people (whether office meetings or in social situations), better luck should continuously come your way.

BE SURE TO CARRY A COMPASS WITH YOU WHEREVER YOU GO.

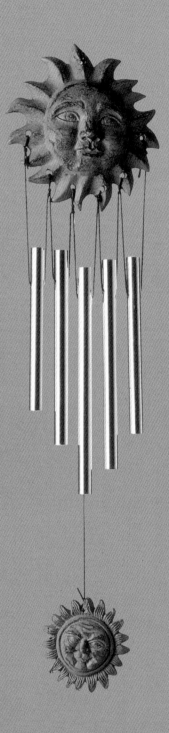

3

THE NINE ASPIRATIONS FORMULA

This formula is the easiest and therefore one of the most popular methods of Feng Shui. It does not require any quantitative calculations and is based entirely on assigned attributes to the nine sectors of the Lo Shu grid. Each corner of the Lo Shu grid relates specifically to an aspiration – ranging from wealth and relationship luck to education, health, and family luck – and also to one of the five elements. The beauty of this formula is its simplicity: by matching the appropriate element with the aspiration of your choice you can immediately start to enhance your potential. Energize one aspiration, or look to all nine; you can work on whatever you desire and be confident of attaining it.

The Nine Aspirations

Because the Nine Aspirations Formula does not require any quantitative calculations and is based entirely on assigned attributes to the nine sectors of the Lo Shu grid, it is relatively easy to put into practice. The first thing to do is to learn which aspiration is associated with which corner of the Lo Shu square: these relate to the eight directions around the outside of the square as well as the central square, which pertains directly to the center of the home, or family luck.

IDENTIFYING THE NINE ASPIRATION CORNERS

The nine aspirations are success in career, love, education, patronage, recognition, attaining prosperity, having a long and healthy life, having good descendants luck, and having family luck.

The formula is simplified by assigning each aspiration to a sector in the Lo Shu grid. It is then easy to identify the corner of a home that corresponds to the aspiration identified. The center is associated with family luck. Each aspiration can be enhanced or energized by focusing on the relevant sector and magnifying the energies of its element (described overleaf).

APPLYING THE FORMULA

WEALTH LUCK: SOUTHEAST

Wealth and prosperity luck is associated with the southeast location of any space. Thus the southeast of any room, home, office, hall, or shopping complex is considered to represent the wealth corner.

RECOGNITION LUCK: SOUTH

This refers to the luck that comes with having a good and honorable name. At its zenith, this kind of luck brings fame and fortune, respect, and high honors. Those in professions requiring mass appeal and popularity will benefit from this kind of luck.

MARRIAGE/RELATIONSHIP LUCK: SOUTHWEST

This aspiration encompasses a range of emotional attachments. It can be energized to have a good marriage or to bring marriage opportunities to those who are single. It can also improve your social luck.

4 SOUTHEAST Small EARTH Prosperity luck	9 SOUTH FIRE Recognition and fame luck	2 SOUTHWEST Big EARTH Love, marriage, and relationship luck
3 EAST Big WOOD Health and longevity luck	5 CENTER EARTH Family luck	7 WEST Small METAL Descendants or children luck
8 NORTHEAST Small EARTH Education luck	1 NORTH WATER Career luck	6 NORTHWEST Big METAL Patronage luck

LUCK FOR A PARTICULAR ASPIRATION CAN BE INCREASED BY ENHANCING THE ELEMENT IN A SPECIFIC SECTOR OF THE HOME, SINCE EACH ASPIRATION IS ASSOCIATED WITH A SPECIFIC LOCATION AND WITH A SPECIFIC ELEMENT.

DESCENDANTS LUCK: WEST

The element of this part of the home may be activated and its energies magnified for good luck and good fortune relating to the next generation. If you cannot have children, it is advisable to activate this corner. If you have children, it is good to activate this corner so that they enjoy the Feng Shui that directly benefits them.

PATRONAGE LUCK: NORTHWEST

This aspiration is represented by the northwest, which is also the place of the patriarch. The trigram placed here is Chien, which symbolizes the leader of the family. Chien also symbolizes heaven, which is why this part of the home is considered one of the most important places. To start with, the toilet or kitchen should never take up too much of the northwest corner of the home. This has a negative effect on the luck of the breadwinner of the household.

CAREER LUCK: NORTH

When main doors are located here it is considered auspicious simply because career success in the old days usually meant holding high office in the emperor's service. From a Feng Shui perspective, good career luck means power and influence. If you are a politician or a corporate person this corner should be activated.

CAREER SUCCESS CAN BE ENHANCED BY ENERGIZING THE ELEMENT LOCATED IN THE NORTH.

EDUCATION LUCK: NORTHEAST

This type of luck benefits those engaged in a course of study or research. In old China, such people often went on to carve out lucrative careers for themselves in the emperor's court. The key to their success lay in doing well in the Imperial exams. Feng Shui thus directly addresses the luck of personal development.

STUDENTS AND RESEARCHERS CAN BENEFIT FROM THE EDUCATION LUCK OF THE NORTHEAST.

HEALTH AND LONGEVITY LUCK: EAST

Living a healthy life to a ripe old age is considered one of the most important manifestations of good fortune. It means one has the luck to see descendants prosper and bring honors to the family name.

FAMILY LUCK: THE CENTER

The center of the home has no trigram since it is seen as the heart of the home. Activating it requires continuous Yang energy, so it should never be left vacant and no toilet or kitchen should be placed there. Ideally, the family or dining room should be here. This will create auspicious togetherness luck for the family – harmony among siblings and between the spouses. When family luck is missing, quarrels are a frequent feature.

Matching the Five Elements

The easiest way of energizing each of the nine sectors of your home is to match the element of the corner that you wish to activate with appropriate objects, shapes, or colors, placing them in the appropriate sector. If you want to energize all nine of the aspirations it is perfectly acceptable to be greedy. You can have it all by energizing every sector of your home, but don't over-energize any one sector by having too much of the element. This creates imbalance.

FOR THE SOUTHEAST AND EAST: USE PLANTS

The southeast brings wealth and the east brings good family relationships and good health. These are the wood sectors and the best representative of wood are plants because they signify the intrinsic nature of this element. Wood is the only one of the five elements that has a life of its own. Thus living plants are the best objects to be placed in these sectors. But choose healthy plants with flowers or broad, succulent leaves. It is acceptable to use fake silk plants, artificial plants are better than dried plants since dried plants represent deathly Yin energy, which can be harmful.

You can also use blue wallpaper, carpets, or soft furnishings since blue is representative of water. This symbolically "produces wood." A mixture of blue and green is excellent for either of these corners.

WATCHPOINT

Avoid cacti or stunted bonsai plants.

PLANTS ARE THE BEST REPRESENTATIVE OF THE WOOD ELEMENT BECAUSE THEY SIGNIFY THE INTRINSIC NATURE OF THIS ELEMENT. REMEMBER TO CHOOSE ONLY HEALTHY PLANTS WITH FLOWERS OR BROAD SUCCULENT LEAVES.

FOR THE SOUTHWEST, NORTHEAST, AND CENTER: USE CRYSTALS AND PEBBLES

The southwest brings love, romance, and good relationships; the northeast brings good education luck, and the center affects the family. These three sectors are symbolic of the earth element and placing natural quartz crystals in these areas creates harmonious energy. Feng Shui is a manifestation of the luck from the earth and the earth element is believed to signify abundance. Crystals symbolize the ultimate essence of the earth element, and pebbles, boulders, ceramics, clay, granite, and glass, as well as anything that comes from the ground, all represent the earth element. Thus placing objects made from any of these materials will create harmonious Feng Shui energies in these sectors.

In the cycle of the five elements, fire produces earth. Thus any item containing red combined with yellows, ocher, or orange are

water (black) and metal (white) has a harmonious relationship because metal produces water. It is also excellent to combine metallic colors with blue or black in the north part of the home.

FOR THE SOUTH: POSITION LIGHTS

The fire element in the south corner brings recognition, luck, respect, and fame, and the best representations of the fire element are bright lights and crystal chandeliers. Create a warm glow in the south part of your home – paint the walls a warm peach or maroon, hang muted shades of red curtains, or even paint the doors bright red. This energizes the corner, bringing fame luck and good name to the family. In my south corner I place a crystal bowl with three lots of Christmas lights that I keep turned on throughout the year. I do not have one light but hundreds activating my south sector.

Furnishings can be combinations of green and red. These colors work well together from a Feng Shui perspective. If you feel that bright green and red is too Christmassy, tone them down by choosing your combination of shades carefully. Colors do not need to be bright to energize the element they represent.

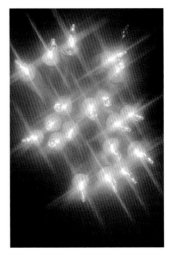

CHRISTMAS LIGHTS MAY BE USED TO CREATE A WARM GLOW IN THE SOUTH PART OF YOUR HOME ALL YEAR ROUND.

excellent for the earth sectors. Use these shades for all your soft furnishings. A red carpet here is excellent and will harmonize brilliantly with decorative objects incorporating a warm earth color.

FOR THE NORTH: USE WATER FEATURES

Water features in the north sector bring career luck, but for Feng Shui purposes they should never be too large because the *I Ching* warns against water rising to its zenith and overflowing. Too much water is like the Yangtze Kiang flooding its banks, bringing death, destruction, and suffering. However, used in small doses and in an elegant manner, water brings enormous good fortune because it is also symbolic of money.

In the north of the home, place a small pond, a tiny fountain, an aquarium, or the painting of a water scene. If you have large grounds and gardens, placing an artificial waterfall in this location brings a lot of good luck. The water flow should always be toward the home and never away from the home. When water flows away from the home, it means that money flows out too.

Furnishings in the north part of the home or just the north wall of living rooms can be in black and white. This is an excellent combination of colors since

FOR THE WEST AND NORTHWEST: USE METAL WIND CHIMES

The west brings good children's luck and the northwest affects the luck of the patriarch. In Feng Shui, wind chimes serve two purposes – they press down on bad luck and they energize good luck. Wind chimes are brilliant Feng Shui tools, but it is as Feng Shui energizers that they are so valuable. This is because they express the movements of the wind and their tinkling sounds create additional Yang energy that activates the energy even more. In the west, hang a seven-rod hollow wind chime in order to attract descendants luck, and in the northwest, hang a slightly larger six-rod hollow metal wind chime.

Wind chimes made of precious metals work even better. Gold or silver wind chimes represent the bounty of the earth and bring tremendous good fortune. When chimes are placed in the northwest, your contacts will bring you so many benefits it is like striking gold.

Furnishings in these two sectors of the home should be in all shades and combinations of white and metallic colors. Earth tones are also excellent when matched with white.

EARTH TONES ARE EXCELLENT FENG SHUI WHEN MATCHED WITH WHITE, SOMETHING WORTH BEARING IN MIND WHEN REDECORATING YOUR HOUSE.

WHEN WIND CHIMES ARE PLACED IN THE NORTHWEST YOU WILL RECEIVE MANY BENEFITS – GOOD LUCK WILL BE ENERGIZED, AND BAD LUCK WILL BE DIMINISHED.

SUPPLEMENTING ELEMENT ENERGIZERS

You can supplement element energizers with techniques that bring Yang energy into the home. Identify the aspirations that mean the most to you and enhance the Yang energy in those sectors alone. It is not advisable to do this in every sector; in Feng Shui it is vital not to overdo things. Too much Yang energy becomes excessive and the family will not be able to tolerate this excess – we Chinese say that one suffers too much heat. Besides, when Yang energy is all over the place and Yin energy becomes displaced, there is imbalance, which leads to the nonexistence of Yang energy – a most inauspicious situation.

Once you have decided which of the aspirations are most important to you, bring in Yang energy using any of the following methods:

- In the east, southeast, southwest, northeast, center, and south use bright lights and crystal chandeliers. Lights in the east and southeast help luck to blossom. Everywhere else they bring good fortune in the form of opportunities.

- In the west and northwest, continuously play music. Have the radio or TV switched on.

- In the east, southeast, or north, keep fish or tortoises.

- In any part of the home, keeping a pet introduces Yang energy. A dog or a cat represents the life force and this is very Yang. This method is suitable for homes that are left vacant for the most part of the day.

KEEP FISH IN THE EAST, SOUTHEAST, OR NORTH TO
ENHANCE THE YANG ENERGY IN THOSE SECTORS.

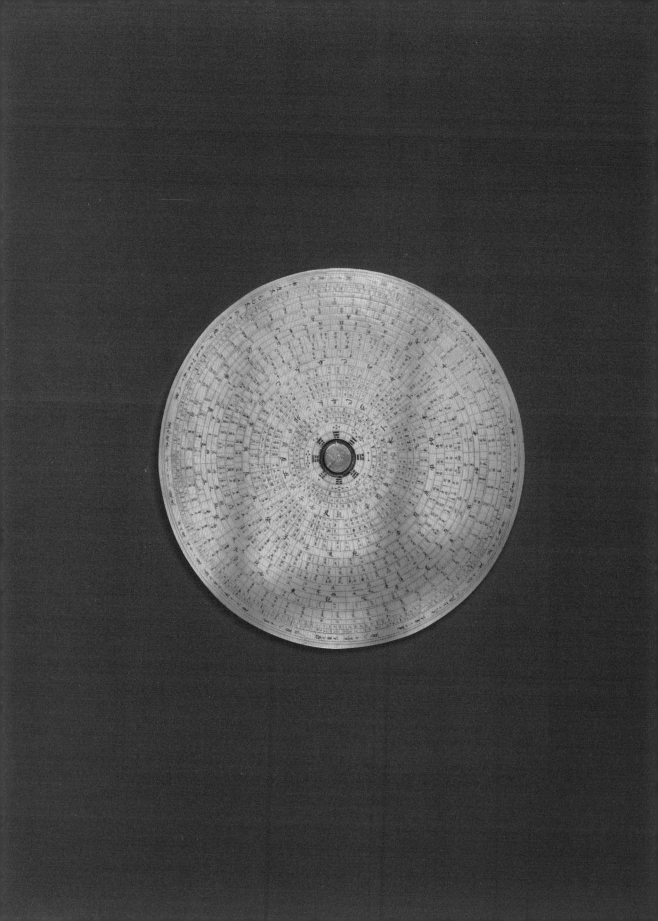

4

THE FLYING STAR FORMULA

The Flying Star Formula represents fairly advanced Feng Shui and can be a little more complex than other formulas. In this chapter you will find step-by-step sequences and tables that are designed to help you understand this important formula. Based on the Lo Shu grid, the formula addresses the time dimension of Feng Shui. It focuses on how to compute and read the natal chart of a home, which reveals auspicious and inauspicious sectors in any home during any particular time. There are precalculated Flying Star charts with detailed notes and these go a long way toward helping the amateur practitioner understand and use this extremely powerful formula.

Cycles of Time

Flying Star Feng Shui is a divinitive science that addresses the cycles of time, which define a home's good and bad luck periods. In an average lifetime, a person lives through about four periods of 20 years each. Every period represents either good or ill fortune. The Flying Star Formula charts the luck of homes according to these cycles of time. The formula is thus based on when any building was first constructed or last renovated.

In Flying Star, or Fey Sin, Feng Shui, the time periods of luck are viewed as cycles, with each cycle lasting 180 years. Each cycle has nine periods, and each period lasts twenty years. According to the Tong Shu or Chinese Almanac, we are in the lower period of the present 180-year cycle, which ends in the year 2043. At the same time, each twenty-year period has a reigning number, and in the current period the reigning number is 7.

THE CURRENT 180-YEAR CYCLE

UPPER PERIOD

1864 to 1883   reigning number 1
1884 to 1903   reigning number 2
1904 to 1923   reigning number 3

MIDDLE PERIOD

1924 to 1943   reigning number 4
1944 to 1963   reigning number 5
1964 to 1983   reigning number 6

LOWER PERIOD

1984 to 2003   reigning number 7 (this is the present period)
2004 to 2023   reigning number 8 (this is the immediate future period)
2024 to 2043   reigning number 9 (this is the longer-term future period)

The reigning number of each of the twenty-year periods, from 1 to 9, is that which is placed in the center of the magical Lo Shu square. The resulting rearrangement of the numbers of the square is the start of Flying Star Feng Shui analysis.

THE LO SHU GRID IN FLYING STAR FENG SHUI

From the placement of the reigning number of any given period, the remaining eight numbers are then allotted their place in the grid based on the sequence of numbers of the original Lo Shu square. This movement of the numbers is referred to as *flying*, and the numbers themselves are known as the *stars*, hence the name Flying Star Feng Shui.

The sequence of flight is all-important and it is useful to understand how the Feng Shui master practitioners calculate the movement of these Flying Stars. The simple first step is to look at two Lo Shu grids – the original Lo Shu grid with the number 5 in the center and the Lo Shu grid of the present period with the number 7 in the center (*see* opposite).

The original Lo Shu square is said to have been brought up the Lo River in about 2205 B.C.E. by a celestial turtle. The numbers on the original square were based on dots found on the back of the turtle. This series of dots was arranged in a pattern of numbers in

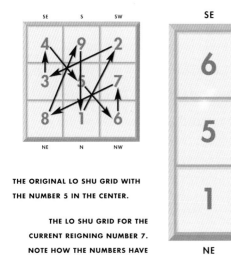

THE ORIGINAL LO SHU GRID WITH THE NUMBER 5 IN THE CENTER.

THE LO SHU GRID FOR THE CURRENT REIGNING NUMBER 7. NOTE HOW THE NUMBERS HAVE BEEN REARRANGED.

SE	S	SW
6	2	4
5	7	9
1	3	8
NE	N	NW

Flying Star Feng Shui can predict severe illnesses of people occupying certain rooms when bad stars will cause illnesses to manifest at specific times. It can predict accidents and deaths. Flying Star Feng Shui is also able to predict the birth of children, the marriages of children of a household, as well as the celebration of longevity birthdays. These latter occasions – births, marriages, and longevity birthdays – are said to be the high happiness occasions of one's life, defining good Feng Shui at its happiest. Flying Star Feng Shui reveals the timing of these happy occasions – but only to those adept at interpreting the way the stars (numbers) interact with each other.

Flying Star Feng Shui is one of the most advanced of the Feng Shui formulas to put into practice. To successfully use this formula there are four steps:

1 Learn how to successfully cast the natal chart of a home.

2 Know the Lo Shu grids of each year according to the Chinese calendar.

3 Interpret the meanings of the star or number combinations in the natal chart and the calendar.

THE FLIGHT PATH OF THE FLYING STARS OR NUMBERS REVEALS A SIGN THAT RESEMBLES THE HEBREW SIGIL OF SATURN.

4 In the case of afflicted or bad stars, know what to do to counter the bad luck. Each area is discussed later in this chapter.

a three-by-three sector grid. Whichever way the numbers were added – horizontally, vertically, or diagonally – they came to 15. The number 15 is significant in that it takes this number of days for the moon to wax or wane in a cycle.

Look at the original grid. See how the numbers move or fly around the grid in a certain sequence. Note how the numbers move in ascending order; their "flight path" forms a shape which also resembles the Sigil of Saturn sign (right). This is the main key to unlocking the secrets of the Flying Star Formula. The three-number sequence adding up to 15 does not continue to apply on subsequent rearranged Lo Shu numbers. This is because when the center number of the Lo Shu changes, so do all the other numbers.

Flying Star Feng Shui is extremely popular in Hong Kong, Taiwan, and Malaysia, and the best exponents of this school come from these areas. Flying Star Feng Shui is divinitive in that an expert is able to develop complex Flying Stars diagrams and from these predict the exact timing of tragic events and happy occasions.

Computing the Natal Chart

Computing the natal chart is complicated and time-consuming, but it reveals many things about the luck potential of your home. The natal chart is a goldmine of information, which, if tapped successfully, can bring enormous prosperity and help householders escape some bad luck and fatal illnesses and accidents. To aid the amateur practitioner, the following pages contain step-by-step sequences and practical examples.

1 DETERMINING THE PERIOD

1 *Find out the year when your home was built. This determines the period and its reigning number, which in turn determines the relevant Lo Shu grid (see pages 58–59). Once you have the relevant reigning number you will be able to create the basic grid. For example, if a house was built between 1964 and 1983 the reigning number would be 6.*

2 *Establish whether the home has been extensively renovated (or redecorated, since redecoration may also be seen as renovation – see box right). So, if the house built between 1964 and 1983 was renovated after 1983, the reigning number has become 7.*

THE FIRST STAGE OF COMPUTING THE NATAL CHART IS TO FIND OUT WHEN YOUR HOME WAS BUILT; THEN YOU CAN FIND OUT ITS REIGNING NUMBER.

DEFINITIONS OF RENOVATION

According to Feng Shui masters, determining what constitutes a renovation is important because it causes the reigning number of the home to change. In Hong Kong, renovation is defined as the home having had roof and walls demolished to make way for new walls and a new roof. In Malaysia, a well-known expert on Flying Stars tells me that when a home is repainted and if there is some banging and construction, it qualifies as renovation. In short, redecoration is also accepted as renovation.

THE LO SHU GRIDS FOR THE NINE REIGNING NUMBERS

The Lo Shu grids for each of the nine reigning numbers are shown opposite. Note the numerals contained in the center (the reigning number for the year) as well as in each of the other sectors. In the Lo Shu squares, the convention always has south placed in the top center grid. When the period changes, the center number changes as do each of the numbers in the other eight squares. The next period change takes place in the lunar new year in 2004. The new period will have 8 as the center ruling number.

THE LO SHU GRID FOR REIGNING NUMBER 1

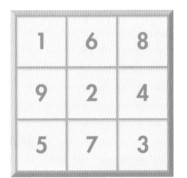

THE LO SHU GRID FOR REIGNING NUMBER 2

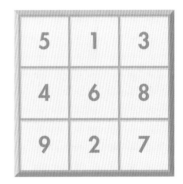

THE LO SHU GRID FOR REIGNING NUMBER 3

THE LO SHU GRID FOR REIGNING NUMBER 4

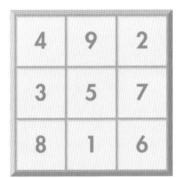

THE LO SHU GRID FOR REIGNING NUMBER 5

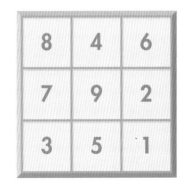

THE LO SHU GRID FOR REIGNING NUMBER 6

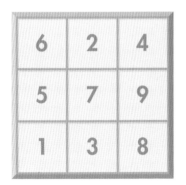

THE LO SHU GRID FOR REIGNING NUMBER 7

THE LO SHU GRID FOR REIGNING NUMBER 8

THE LO SHU GRID FOR REIGNING NUMBER 9

2 DETERMINING THE EXACT DIRECTION AND LOCATION OF THE MAIN DOOR

The next step for computing your home's natal chart is to take an accurate reading of the direction of the main door, as described on pages 22–23. You must also accurately demarcate and superimpose the nine-sector Lo Shu grid onto the layout of your home (*see* page 25). The numbers on the Lo Shu grid are now known as the main star numerals.

In Flying Star Feng Shui main door directions and locations can also mean the general orientation of the house, and each different master practitioner stresses a different interpretation. Thus when taking the direction of the main door, it is vital to consider the four main options now being used (and taught) by the different masters. These are summarized as follows:

1 Some consider the general orientation of the home, i.e. where it is facing as a whole.

2 Some consider the most Yang side, i.e. where there is the most activity, such as the main road, the highway, or where there is most noise.

3 Some consider the place that receives the most light, i.e. where most of the windows of the home are facing.

4 Some masters consider the direction the main door is facing (inside looking out).

TAKING AN ACCURATE READING OF THE DIRECTION YOUR MAIN DOOR FACES IS AN IMPORTANT STEP IN CALCULATING THE NATAL CHART FOR YOUR HOME.

I prefer to use the last criterion, because it is the most straightforward.

3 DETERMINING THE PLACEMENT OF WATER AND MOUNTAIN STARS

The main door direction determines the water and mountain star numbers that are placed in the center grid on the right and left of the main star numeral respectively.

The water star is described as the *facing star* or *siang sin*, and the mountain star is described as the *sitting star* or *chor sin*.

1 *Take your established door direction and relate it to the appropriate number on the relevant Lo Shu grid. For example, in the home whose reigning number is 7 and where the main door faces east, the number that will become the water star is 5.*

2 *Write a small 5 just to the right of the main star number 7 in the center of your natal chart.*

3 *The mountain star is determined by looking at the main number that is directly opposite the direction where the main door is located. In this case, it is the main number 9.*

4 *Write a small 9 just to the left of the main star number 7 in the center of your natal chart.*

The water star is said to be auspicious if it has the numbers 1, 6, or 8. In this period of 7, the number 7 is also regarded as auspicious. Usually these numbers are considered to mean wealth and prosperity if they can be properly and correctly enhanced, as described on pages 72–87.

The mountain star is said to be the sitting star. It is always considered to be opposite to the water star, which is said to be the facing star.

SOUTH

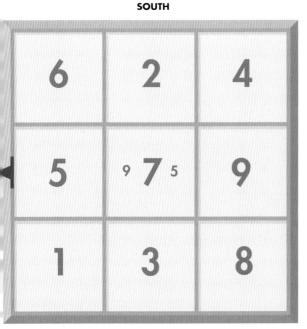

NORTH

THE NUMBER 7 IS THE REIGNING NUMBER OF THE CURRENT PERIOD AND IS PLACED IN THE CENTER OF THE LO SHU GRID. THE WATER STAR (SMALL 5) IS POSITIONED TO ITS RIGHT AND THE MOUNTAIN STAR (SMALL 9) TO ITS LEFT.

Consequently, if the mountain star is in the north, then it is said to be sitting in the north and facing south. If it is in the east, then it is sitting in the east and facing west.

The mountain star is also said to be auspicious if it carries the auspicious numbers 1, 6, 7, or 8.

4 DETERMINING THE REST OF THE WATER STAR NUMERALS

With the center numerals in place for all three of the stars of the natal chart – the main star, the water star, and the mountain star – the next step will be to determine how each of the water stars flies around the Lo Shu grid.

1 *To begin, please note that the flight path of both the secondary stars follows the main star numeral. This means that the stars fly from sector to sector in the grid according to the Sigil of Saturn movement shown on page 59. So we know, for example, that the next location after 7 for both the water and mountain stars will be in the sector where the main star numeral is 8, or in this case the northwest sector. After that it will be where the main star numeral is 9, i.e. the west sector, and so on.*

2 *What we need to know is what the water star number will be in the northwest sector and subsequently in the rest of the other sectors. This is determined according to whether the water star flies in a positive or a negative manner. A positive flight means the numbers will be ascending as it flies. A negative flight path means the numbers will be descending as it flies. To determine whether the flight is positive or negative for the water star, return once again to the main door to determine exactly what direction it faces.*

3 *Divide each of the cardinal and secondary compass directions into three subdirections, making a total of 24 subdirections. When you take the direction of your door, check whether the door is facing subdirection 1, 2, or 3 of the particular direction.*

4 For main doors located in one of the cardinal directions: *based on the original Lo Shu, the numbers of the four cardinal directions are odd. So, for example, south is 9, north is 1, east is 3, and west is 7.*

For all odd numbers, the movement of the water star is plus, minus, minus (+ – –) for the three subdirections. In the example here, the main door faces east, so it is an odd number. As a result:

• If the door is facing the first subdirection, the flight of the water star will be positive and the numbers will be ascending, i.e. from 5 to 6 to 7 and so on.

• If the main door faces the second or third subdirection, the movement of the water star will be negative and the numbers will be descending, i.e. from 5 to 4 to 3 and so on.

In the example shown opposite the water star moves in a positive way because the main door faces the first subdirection of east. The natal chart with the water stars in place is shown here.

5 For main doors located in one of the secondary directions: *again based on the original Lo Shu, the equivalent numbers are even. Thus the southeast is 4, the southwest is 2, the northeast is 8, and the northwest is 6. For all even numbers, the movement for the water star is minus, plus, plus (– + +). This means that:*

• If the main door is facing any of the secondary directions and it is in the first subsector, the movement of the water star is descending, i.e., from 5 to 4 to 3 and so on.

• If the door is facing the second or third subdirec-

tions, the movement is ascending, e.g., from 5 to 6 to 7.

I supply precalculated tables and give an analysis of each variation for the period of 7 on pages 72–87. But before looking at these it is important to understand how the charts can be read.

5 DETERMINING THE REST OF THE MOUNTAIN STAR NUMERALS

Whether the mountain star numerals ascend or descend during their flight around the natal chart is determined according to whether its center number is odd or even.

1 *If the center number is odd, the flying sequence is plus, minus, minus (+––). This means the numbers will be ascending if the main door direction is facing the first subdirection, and will be descending if the main door direction is facing the second or third subdirections. Once again, therefore, the direction of the main door is crucial. In the example, the main door is facing the first subdirection of*

DIRECTIONS ACCORDING TO COMPASS READINGS					
	BEARING (DEGREES)		BEARING (DEGREES)		BEARING (DEGREES)
South 1	157.5–172.5	South 2	172.5–187.5	South 3	187.5–202.5
North 1	337.5–352.5	North 2	352.5–007.5	North 3	007.5–022.5
East 1	067.5–082.5	East 2	082.5–097.5	East 3	097.5–112.5
West 1	247.5–262.5	West 2	262.5–277.5	West 3	277.5–292.5
Southwest 1	202.5–217.5	Southwest 2	217.5–232.5	Southwest 3	232.5–247.5
Southeast 1	112.5–127.5	Southeast 2	127.5–142.5	Southeast 3	142.5–157.5
Northeast 1	022.5–037.5	Northeast 2	037.5–052.5	Northeast 3	052.5–067.5
Northwest 1	292.5–307.5	Northwest 2	307.5–322.5	Northwest 3	322.5–337.5

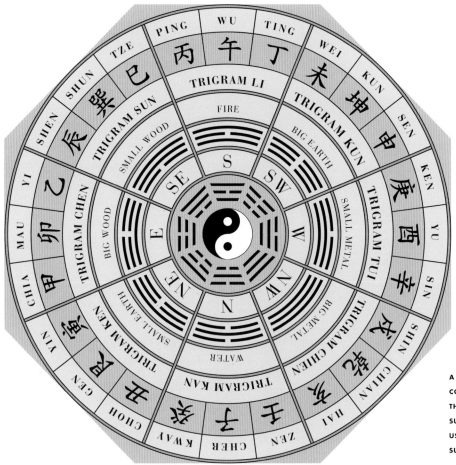

east and the center number is odd. So the flight of the mountain star is positive and therefore ascending. Consult the completed natal chart, below right.

2 *If the center numeral of the mountain star is even, the sequence will be minus, plus, plus (− + +). Consequently, if the main door direction is facing the*

first subdirection, the numerals will fly in a descending order, and if the door direction is facing the second or third subdirection, the numeral will move in an ascending fashion.

	SE	S	SW	
	8 **6** 4	4 **2** 9	6 **4** 2	
NE	7 **5** 3	9 **7** 5	2 **9** 7	NW
	3 **1** 8	5 **3** 1	1 **8** 6	
	NE	N	NW	

THE WATER STAR NUMERALS
MOVE IN A POSITIVE WAY,
INDICATING THAT THE MAIN
DOOR FACES THE FIRST
SUBDIRECTION OF EAST.

6 READING THE NATAL CHARTS

The combined star numbers in each of the nine grids offer detailed readings on the luck of each of the nine sectors of any home. The interpretation of these numbers is what Flying Star Feng Shui is all about, and how good a master is at interpreting these numbers determines his level of experience.

- **The numbers in each sector and their combinations.** There are 81 combinations of numbers, and different periods show a preponderance of certain number combinations. Also the combinations have varying degrees of good and bad luck in different periods. What is good luck in the period of 7 may be bad luck in the period of 8. Thus, for example, the double 7 (where both the mountain and water stars are 7) is deemed most auspicious in this current period of 7, but they turn malevolent and most unfortunate when we enter into the period of 8 in February 2004.

- **Their corresponding elements and how these elements interact with the element of the grid they fly into.** For example, the number 9 (fire) flying into east (wood) would bring bad luck to the east since the fire destroys the wood. But the number 1 (water) flying into southeast (wood) is good because water produces wood.

- **Whether they are mountain or water stars.** For example, if the mountain star flies into a sector where there is a wall or a mountain nearby, this would be lucky, but if there was a pond there it would be most unlucky if the mountain star had an auspicious number. If the mountain star had an inauspicious number and it fell into water, then the bad luck would be deemed to have been remedied!

THE NUMBERS 1, 6, 7, OR 8 APPEARING IN THE SECTOR WHERE YOUR FRONT DOOR IS LOCATED WILL BRING YOU GOOD LUCK.

Once you know what your Flying Star chart looks like you will be able to understand why you may be enjoying a certain type of good fortune or why you have been undergoing a period of misfortunes, illness, or accidents.

1 *Apply Flying Star Feng Shui analysis to your home by tracing the relevant chart from page 61 and superimposing it onto your house plan, as described on pages 24–25. Try to be accurate and make sure the plan is drawn to scale.*

2 *Usually this kind of Feng Shui analysis applies to the whole building or house rather than to individual rooms. Those living in apartments should use Flying Star analysis on their whole apartment floor plans. However, energizing good stars can apply to individual rooms.*

3 *You can base your analysis of the numbers on the table on pages 70–71. Further analysis can be based on the cycles and interactions of the elements.*

MAIN DOOR LOCATION

Check how many of the lucky numbers 1, 6, 7, or 8 you have in the sector where the main door is. If all the three numbers appearing in the sector are auspicious, it means the sector is great for the main door. If, on the other hand, the numbers are inauspicious (5 or 2), then the main door is said to be afflicted for this entire period up to the year 2004, unless after 2004 you renovate the home, thereby making it a period of 8 home.

To counteract the negative effect of Flying Stars, there are several things you can try:

• You can work through the formula and come up with a more auspicious main door location, although this means moving the main door and relocating it to a more auspicious location. Sometimes just changing the direction from the first to the second subdirection can solve the problem since this changes the flight of the water and mountain stars.

• You can investigate the unlucky numbers in detail. Thus, if the water star has the unlucky 2 or 5, press it down by placing a large metal object near the main door. If the mountain star has the 2 or 5, put a water feature there to "drown the mountain." Still water works best in this situation.

MAIN BEDROOM LOCATION

If any of the bedrooms is afflicted by the number 5 illness star or worse – by having double 5s or 5 and 2 or double 2s – the advice is to move the occupant to

WATCHPOINT

Counteract the negative effect of the 2 or 5 of a mountain star with a water feature near the main door.

IF 2 AND 5 APPEAR IN ANY SECTOR OCCUPIED BY A BEDROOM, TRY CHANGING THE DOOR DIRECTION OR USING A SIX-ROD WIND CHIME TO SUPPRESS THE NEGATIVE ENERGY.

another room immediately. A double 5 means severe illness leading possibly to death. For example, heart problems, cancer, or the diagnosis of AIDS can be exacerbated by the presence of the double 5. A gathering of 2s and 5s always spells disaster, severe loss, fatal accidents, or chronic illnesses.

If you see a 2 and 5 in any sector that is occupied by a bedroom, it is best to move occupants out of that bedroom and use the place as a storeroom. If you cannot do this, try to manipulate the Flying Star chart by using another door or changing the door direction. If you cannot use either of these two options then try hanging a six-rod wind chime to press down on the fatal 5s and 2s. Wind chimes that have six rods are a powerful way of controlling inauspicious Flying Stars.

The Meanings of the Numbers

Applying Flying Star Feng Shui to bring good fortune and dissolve bad luck requires experience in interpreting the meanings of the numbers and their combinations in each square. Below I explain the value of pairs and triplets of the same good luck number – 1, 6, 7, 8, or 9 – in a square. Overleaf a table shows how the different combinations of the mountain and water stars affect the home. If the effect is bad, there are ways of improving the luck, and if the effect is good, there are further ways of enhancing the energy.

I cannot hope to explain everything about Flying Star Feng Shui in this book but if you understand the good and bad meanings of numbers you will be able to avert very bad Feng Shui. This should be sufficient as a supplementary tool to the practice of other Feng Shui techniques. In other words, you should endeavor to use Flying Star Feng Shui as a defensive tool against inauspicious time dimension Feng Shui.

IF TRIPLE 6s OCCUR IN THE SECTOR WHERE YOUR MAIN DOOR IS LOCATED YOUR CHILDREN WILL BECOME GREAT SCHOLARS.

THE AUSPICIOUS TRIPLES AND DOUBLES

According to the texts on Flying Star Feng Shui there are certain numbers that, when they occur as triples or doubles, signify extreme good fortune. This good fortune takes many forms and does not always mean wealth and prosperity alone. Good fortune can mean having many sons, excellent health, honor brought to the family, or one's power and influence being magnified and enhanced.

Double 1s promise a brilliant generation, and good fortune will continue for sixty years. Double 1s are an auspicious indication in Flying Star Feng Shui, especially when they occur in the north sector. This is because the number 1 is the number of the north. Enhance with water and watch your career take off.

Triple 6s occurring in the sector where the main door is located mean great wealth. Your children will become great scholars. If you have three sons, one of them will have a distinguished career in the armed forces. If you have a triple 6 occurring in your Flying Star chart, enhance that sector with a six-rod wind chime. Do not have toilets or kitchens in sectors that have the triple 6, since this kills off all the good fortune.

Double 7s are a combination that spells superb money luck during the period 7. Again, if you have such a sector, make sure you locate an important room here. Period 7 Flying Star charts have this occurrence where the main door has the double 7. But in the next period, the double 7 becomes very unlucky. Change the door direction before the period changes.

DOUBLE 7s SPELL SUPERB MONEY LUCK DURING THE PERIOD 7. TRY AND LOCATE AN IMPORTANT ROOM IN THIS SECTOR.

Double 8s are a potent combination in the northeast sector. Such a home will produce powerful children who will bring prosperity and honor to the family. This combination in the sector of the main door brings prosperity for all the family. Money will start to roll in after 2004.

Double 9s in the south bring fame beyond your imagination. This is because in the south the double 9 becomes three 9s, since the south is also 9. It is an extremely favorable combination and especially so for those involved in a political career. Households with this feature in the natal chart will be prosperous and, as with the double 1, this prosperity will continue for at least sixty years.

POWERFUL CHILDREN WHO WILL BRING PROSPERITY AND HONOR TO THE FAMILY WILL BE BORN INTO HOMES WHERE DOUBLE 8s OCCUR IN THE NORTHEAST SECTOR.

THE MEANINGS OF THE STAR COMBINATIONS OF NUMBERS

MOUNTAIN STAR	WATER STAR	INDICATED DIVINATIONS AND OUTCOMES OF THE COMBINATION	ENHANCERS FOR GOOD LUCK COMBINATIONS OR REMEDIES FOR BAD LUCK COMBINATIONS
1	2	Marriage problems and danger of losses Water in mountain is also a sign of grave danger, as is mountain falling into water	Use plants to exhaust the water and strengthen earth element
2	1	The matriarch is too strong leading to marital problems	Use metal to exhaust
1	3	Wealth and fame luck are indicated	Use water to enhance and water plants
3	1	Prosperity luck is so good that if you don't have the karma/luck to live in this home you will change residence	Plant a bamboo grove to strengthen your luck
1	4	Political luck. Media and publicity luck. Romance luck	Use slow-moving water but not too much
4	1	Romance luck but too much water leads to sex scandals. Affairs leading to unhappiness and breakup of family	Position a Kuan Yin statue
1	5	Health problems dealing with kidneys	Use wind chime
5	1	Hearing problems. Sex-related illness	Use wind chime
1	6	Auspicious. Intelligence with great commercial skills	Enhance with metal
6	1	Financial luck and high achievers in the family	Enhance with metal
1	7	Good money luck in period of 7 only; in period of 8 this combination means loss of wealth	Enhance with crystals or gem tree
7	1	Extremely good prosperity luck	Use a water feature
1	8	Excellent wealth luck into 8 period	Enhance with crystals
8	1	Excellent and auspicious luck Money and family luck	Enhance with water
1	9	Good combination but can turn bad when 5 flies in	Do not enhance
9	1	Same as above	Do not disturb
2	3	Arguments and misunderstandings of the most severe kind. Back stabbing, hatred, legal disputes. Inauspicious	Use still water in a large urn or water container to cool tempers Do not play music or hang wind chimes here.
3	2	As bad as above and can get dangerous for those in politics. Tendency to obesity	Some masters recommend gold and fire
2	4	Wives and mothers-in-law quarrel and fight. Disharmony	Use water
4	2	Illness of internal organs – husband has affairs	Use water
2	5	Extremely inauspicious. Total loss and catastrophe	Use plenty of wind chimes. Beware – do not have a fire here or there could be a death; never put kitchen in 2/5
5	2	Misfortunes and extreme bad luck. Illness may be fatal	Use wind chime
2	6	Very easy life of leisure. This auspicious combination is spoiled if a five-rod wind chime is placed here	Use wind chime
6	2	Great affluence and everything successful	No need to enhance
2	7	There is richness and money during the period of 7 but luck of children will not be good since there will be problems conceiving During the period of 8 everything is bad!	Use metal (bells) in period of 7 and use water in period of 8
7	2	Money luck dissipates. Children luck is dimmed	Use wind chime

THE MEANINGS OF THE STAR COMBINATIONS OF NUMBERS

MOUNTAIN STAR	WATER STAR	INDICATED DIVINATIONS AND OUTCOMES OF THE COMBINATION	ENHANCERS FOR GOOD LUCK COMBINATIONS OR REMEDIES FOR BAD LUCK COMBINATIONS
2	8	Richness and wealth but there is ill health, although this is minor and can be remedied	Use water to overcome bad health star
8	2	Better then above. There is money luck	Use mountain principle
2	9	Extremely bad luck. Nothing succeeds unless remedied	Use water plants
9	2	Better luck than above	Use water
3	4	Danger of mental instability. Tendency to stress	Use bright lights
4	3	Emotional stress due to relationship problems	Use red to overcome
3	5	Loss of wealth. Severe cash flow problems. If bedroom is here, financial loss is severe If kitchen is here sickness is inevitable Better not to stay in this part of the house	Exhaust the 5 with metal but not with wind chimes or bells. Use copper mountain
5	3	Money troubles. Disputes. Bad business luck	Use water
3	6	Period of slow growth	Use water
6	3	Unexpected windfall. Speculative luck	Enhance with gemstones
3	7	You will get robbed or burgled. Violence Not so bad in period of 7 but sure to get robbed in period of 8	Use water
7	3	Grave danger of injury to limbs. Be careful	Use water
3	8	Not good for children under 12 years	Use bright lights to cure
8	3	Move children away from this sector	Use red, yellow
4	5	Prone to sexually transmitted diseases Breast cancer	Use water/mountain
5	4	Just as bad as above	Use water/mountain
4	6	Bad luck for women who will bear heavy burden	Strengthen earth element
6	4	Unexpected windfall for women	Enhance with wind chime
4	7	Bad luck in love. Will get cheated by opposite sex	Use water
7	4	Taken for a ride by someone of the opposite sex	Use water
4	8	Bad for very young children	Use lights to combat
8	4	Overpowering matriarch. Love life of younger generation will suffer from the wiles of the mother	Use fire or red to overcome
4	9	A time for preparation. Good for students	Use wood or plants
9	4	Good luck for those starting new business	Use water to enhance
5	7	Problems caused by excessive gossiping. Danger of poisoning or anything to do with the mouth	Use metal in period of 7 and water in period of 8
7	5	Same as for 5/7	
5	8	Problems related to the limbs, joints, and bones of the body. It is necessary to be careful of rough sports	Use water to pacify
8	5	Same as for 5/8	
5	9	Bad luck and tempers. Excessive mental disorder or stress – there is unhappiness	Use wind chime
9	5	Same as for 5/9	
6	7	Sword fighting killing breath	Use water
7	6	Same as for 6/7	
6	8	Wealth, popularity, prosperity. Great richness Probably the best combination in flying star formula	Enhance with water and make sure you have an entrance or window in that sector
8	6	Same as for 6/8	
7	9	Extreme problems during period of 8. All troubles will be caused through excessive vulnerability to sexual advances. There is also danger of fire hazards	Use water or earth (big boulders) to press down on the bad luck
9	7	Same as for 7/9	

Precalculated Flying Star Charts

ere are the precalculated Flying Star charts of all houses and homes, offices and buildings that were (or will be) built or renovated between February 4th, 1984 and February 4th, 2004. This twenty-year period covers the period of 7, so these charts are known as the period of 7 Flying Star charts. There are 16 charts in all, covering 24 door directions as described on page 65. There are 16 Flying Star charts rather than 24 because the subdirections 2 and 3 have the same Flying Star chart.

SOUTH 1

- This house has the excellent double 7 stars in the sector where the front door is located. It is unfortunate that the main star numeral is 2, since this causes some hiccups and obstacles, but generally the door is good. Put a plant near the front door to press down on the inauspicious 2.
- The west sector is very bad. The 5/9 combination creates severe stress and problems for anyone sleeping or working in this sector. Hang a curved knife here to counter these inauspicious stars.
- The best room in the house is the room in the northeast sector where the combination of 1, 6, and 8 stars bring enormous good fortune to anyone staying there. This sector should therefore house the master bedroom.

Main Door Facing South 1

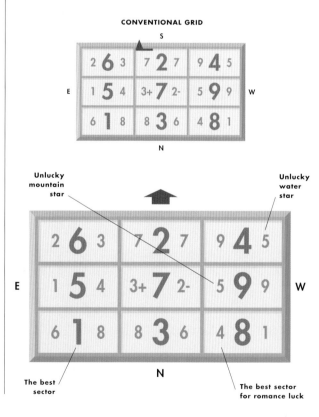

CONVENTIONAL GRID

The best sector

The best sector for romance luck

Unlucky mountain star

Unlucky water star

NOTES

Each Flying Star chart is presented in two different formats:

- First they are presented using the conventional Lo Shu placement of directions where the direction south is placed on top.
- Then, to make analysis easier for readers, these charts have been reoriented such that the main door direction has been placed on top.

Use them over your house plan (see pages 24–25).

Please make sure the toilet or kitchen is not placed in this sector of the house.

- The northwest is the sector with romance luck, and the main numeral being 8 brings money with love.
- In the southwest, the water star is 5 so place a plant here to dissolve the effect of this unlucky 5. If this proves insufficient to overcome the 5/9 combination, use metal to exhaust the strengthened 5 earth energy. In the west, the mountain star is 5, so place a water feature here to counter this unlucky mountain star numeral.

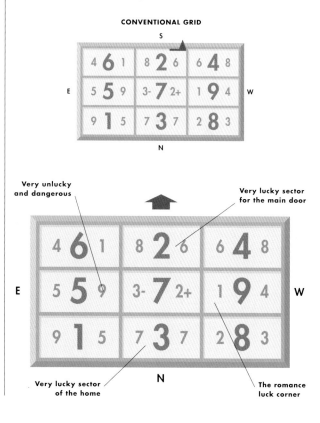

A PLANT NEAR THE SOUTH 1 MAIN DOOR COUNTERACTS BAD LUCK.

especially if it is the master bedroom or study of the breadwinner of the family, then legal entanglements could become a real problem. Try to keep the corner quiet and try to pacify these bad stars with metal and fire combinations and some quiet Yang energy. Keep these two places as quiet as possible. No noise, otherwise quarrels and arguments could well become violent.

- The luckiest grid in the house is the north with the double 7 and the southwest 6/8. You should energize these two sectors and place all your important rooms here.

SOUTH 2 OR 3

- This house has good stars in the grid of the front door with the 6 water star and the 8 mountain star. However, because the direction is south, whose element is fire, placing a water feature here could cause the elements to clash. A water feature is therefore not recommended near the front door. It would also afflict the lucky mountain star, which has the 8 numeral causing the mountain to fall into the water. The best way to energize the 6/8 combination, which means wealth, polarity, and recognition, is to leave it alone.
- There are two 5 numerals in the east grid, indicating a severely afflicted east sector. Do not place anyone in any bedroom in this sector in the period of 7, since the double 5 will cause the ripening of illness karma. Children staying in this sector could succumb to frequent illness. Place a six-rod wind chime or hang a curved knife to exhaust the double 5 of the east grid.
- The northwest and the center are negatively affected by the 3/2 combination of quarrelsome stars. If important rooms are located in the northwest, and

Main Door Facing South 2 or 3

CONVENTIONAL GRID

S

4 **6** 1	8 **2** 6	6 **4** 8
5 **5** 9	3- **7** 2+	1 **9** 4
9 **1** 5	7 **3** 7	2 **8** 3

E (left) W (right)

N

Very unlucky and dangerous

Very lucky sector for the main door

4 **6** 1	8 **2** 6	6 **4** 8
5 **5** 9	3- **7** 2+	1 **9** 4
9 **1** 5	7 **3** 7	2 **8** 3

E (left) W (right)

Very lucky sector of the home

N

The romance luck corner

NORTH 1

- This house has an auspicious front door with the 8 water star and the 6 mountain star. Placing a water feature such as a small waterfall with the water flowing toward the home's front door will bring great prosperity. The back door is also prosperous. Thus for period 7 having a door that is placed north and facing the first subsection of north is very auspicious.

- The quarrelsome sectors are the center of the house and the southeast. Husbands and wives will quarrel incessantly if the master bedroom is placed in these sectors. This is due to the 3/2 combination. The 2/3 of the center is known as stubborn fighting killing sha. This causes disputes, arguments, lawsuits, complaints, back stabbing, and intense hostility from outsiders to befall the residents. Overcome this with small amounts of metal and fire elements (red and gold). Keep the place of the 3/2 very quiet! The 3/2 of the southeast cause disputes in business leading to loss and lawsuits. Overcome this with the fire element (bright lights).

- The northeast and south sectors of this house are very lucky. Put all the important rooms in these parts of the house. The wonderfully lucky combination of 8/6 in the northeast indicates wealth and power. If your bedroom is located in this sector you will enjoy wealth luck. Enhance with earth energy.

- In the south is the auspicious double 7 combination – again very lucky. Indeed, this is extremely lucky in the period of 7 but when the period of 8 comes around this leads to armed robbery! So you are advised to change your main door or back door before 2004.

- The 4/1 combination in the northwest and in the east spells romance/love luck and scholarly achievements. But excessive water in either sector causes sex scandals. Balance is vital. Grow water lilies and lotus to attract the good without the bad.

- The 9/5 and 5/9 combinations in the west and southwest are very dangerous. In very very rare situations this combination brings great wealth luck but often it merely causes severe mental and financial afflictions. Pressure and stress usually result from this combination. Use metal and water concepts to combat this combination.

- This commentary will change for the period of 8, which comes around in 2004.

Main Door Facing North 1

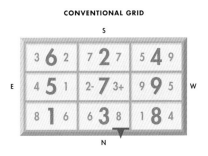

CONVENTIONAL GRID

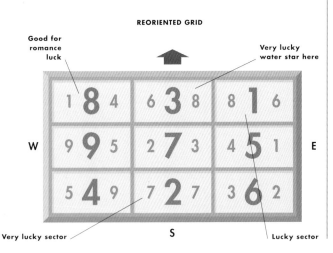

REORIENTED GRID

Good for romance luck

Very lucky water star here

Very lucky sector

Lucky sector

NORTH 2 OR 3

- This house has a very auspicious front door with the double 7 combination. This means that both the water star and the mountain star are auspicious during this period of 7. If you were to build a water feature in full view of the door, the luck of prosperity would come to all residents within the home. The back door is equally auspicious with a 6 mountain star. Therefore, if you were to build a wall behind to support the door, it will be another strong luck feature. Since the back is south and of the fire element, tapping the mountain star is an excellent and fast way to prosperity.
- The main obstacle indicated by the Flying Star chart

METAL OBJECTS CAN COUNTERACT FINANCIAL AND HEALTH PROBLEMS IN THE WEST.

for this house is the severe affliction indicated for family harmony (the center) and for the patriarch (the northwest). Note both locations have the quarrelsome 2/3 combination. This means there will be plenty of shouting, anger, arguments, and disharmony among residents in the household. However, there is also a great deal of money, which should offer some consolation.

- Do not have a bedroom in the east and northeast sectors because there are two number 5s in the east. (Note: the main star numeral and the water star numeral in the east will cause anyone staying in this sector to succumb to severe illness.) Also, the 5/9 combinations in both corners spell severe problems related to health and money. Use metal to exhaust the earth 5, or water might be helpful to overcome it. Different masters recommend different solutions and remedies to counter the 5/9.
- The 1/4 combination in the southeast will cause there to be romance luck associated with money, but if there is a water feature in this corner, romance is of a scandalous nature (e.g. where one or both parties are already married indulging in an illicit union). The 4/1 combination in the west tends to bring romance of a safer kind. Again, there is money in the love luck. Enhance with metal, but do not use wind chimes and let it be quiet metal otherwise the romance will turn scandalous.

Main Door Facing North 2 or 3

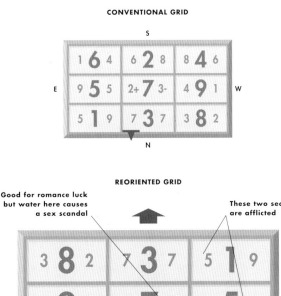

CONVENTIONAL GRID

S

1 6 4	6 2 8	8 4 6
9 5 5	2+ 7 3-	4 9 1
5 1 9	7 3 7	3 8 2

E — W

N

REORIENTED GRID

Good for romance luck but water here causes a sex scandal

These two sectors are afflicted

3 8 2	7 3 7	5 1 9
4 9 1	2 7 3	9 5 5
8 4 6	6 2 8	1 6 4

W — E

S

EAST 1

- In this house the main door is in the east where the main star numeral is 5. Generally for this period of 7, a main door in the east does not bring any luck. But after the year 2004 in the period of 8, luck changes for the better. In the house chart below, however, the water and mountain star numerals of the main door sector add up to 10, and this brings some good news. There will be some months when the luck brought in by the front door is excellent but the luck will not be consistent. Some old books contend that a 3/7 combination at the place of the door indicates residents falling prey to armed robbery or of being cheated. The danger here is to the feet or legs. Those more than 45 years old should be extra careful. There is no cure for this affliction save to avoid using this door.
- The luckiest sector is the northwest, where the three numbers 1, 6, and 8 bring exceptional good luck to anyone staying in that corner of the house. If the master bedroom is located here the patriarch benefits enormously and the luck is extended to the whole family. Place a wealth vase filled with semiprecious stones in this corner to energize and magnify the good fortune of this corner for the breadwinner.
- The other good sectors are the southeast and the northeast, although the luck in these corners is not nearly as serious as in the northwest corner. If a water feature with a single turtle is placed in the north sector this will activate the auspicious water star of the north bringing money and success to the house.
- The 5/1 combination in the north will cause anyone having a bedroom here to have problems related to hearing disabilities and sex diseases. A metal ornament can counter this. Water here is also beneficial.
- The 1/6 combination in the northwest is excellent for education luck and bodes well for children.
- The 2/7 of the west indicates wealth but a lack of children luck. Use metal to control.

Main Door Facing East 1

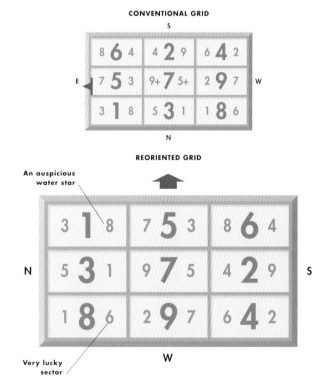

CONVENTIONAL GRID

REORIENTED GRID

An auspicious water star

Very lucky sector

A WEALTH VASE FILLED WITH SEMIPRECIOUS STONES CAN BE PLACED IN THE NORTHWEST SECTOR TO INCREASE THE GOOD LUCK OF THE BREADWINNER.

EAST 2 OR 3

- In this house the main door is also located in the east where the main star numeral 5 causes problems. However, the water star of the main door in this house is the auspicious 7 so a water feature placed here in the east would be lucky for the house. This also makes the bad mountain star 2 fall into the water. Build a small waterfall with the water flowing toward the house (not away from the house).
- The lucky sectors of this house are the southwest and the northeast. In both these sectors the water stars are auspicious because they are of the earth element flying into earth sectors. Thus in the southwest the star numeral 8 enhances the auspicious essence of the sector. If the matriarch of the house stays here it is exceptionally lucky for her. However, the combination of 3/8 could be harmful for children under 12, so it is best if young children are not placed here.

Main Door Facing East 2 or 3

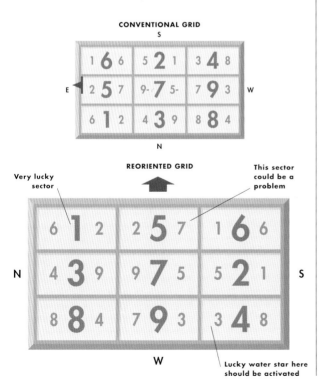

CONVENTIONAL GRID

S

1 6 6	5 2 1	3 4 8
2 5 7	9- 7 5-	7 9 3
6 1 2	4 3 9	8 8 4

E ◀ ▶ W

N

REORIENTED GRID

Very lucky sector

This sector could be a problem

⬆

6 1 2	2 5 7	1 6 6
4 3 9	9 7 5	5 2 1
8 8 4	7 9 3	3 4 8

N ◀ ▶ S

W

Lucky water star here should be activated

A SMALL MOUND IN THE GARDEN MADE UP OF STONES PAINTED GOLD WILL BRING PROSPERITY LUCK IF PLACED IN THE NORTHEAST SECTOR.

- In the northeast, the earth element numeral 2 also enhances this sector's element, and with the numeral 6 mountain star it signifies gold found in the mountain. The main numeral of this grid is 1, which is also a lucky number. This makes the northeast extremely lucky. It is a good idea to energize the sector with a "pretend" mountain of gold. You should be able to simulate this by creating a small mound in the garden made up of stones that have been painted a gold color. This colorfully painted mound will bring prosperity luck. The combination of 2/6 also indicates an affluent and easy life that is enhanced with lots of gold, i.e., metal.
- The combination of 1/6 in the southeast sector indicates residents have great financial skills and high intelligence.
- The south sector with the 5 mountain star and a main star 2 is bad. The center with the 9/5 combination is also bad. Family members will be prone to problems and run the risk of suffering from both illness and disharmony.

WEST 1

- In this house the water star of the main door's sector is the unlucky number 2. However, because this sector is west, and because 2 represents the earth element, it is beneficial. The main door is therefore not seriously afflicted by the 2. The mountain star is the lucky 7 so the main door is lucky and brings income but this combination of 2/7 brings bad luck for children. It is better if they stay away from home.

- The sector of the northwest is especially auspicious. This is the sector of the breadwinner and the 1/6 combination indicates they will have superb financial skills. The water star in this sector is 1, which is extremely auspicious. It means that prosperity luck has arrived. So it is vital to energize the water star with a metal wind chime here. Remember that metal produces water. That the mountain star is the numeral 6 compounds and enhances the luck. On no account should this sector be destroyed by having a toilet or kitchen here. If you do, it is a tremendous waste of good Feng Shui since this is the luckiest part of the house.

- At the back of the house is the east sector with the afflicted 3/7 combination sitting on a 5 main star numeral. The east is especially bad and anyone with a bedroom in this sector will get robbed and mugged. There could even be violence, so move out of there! It is

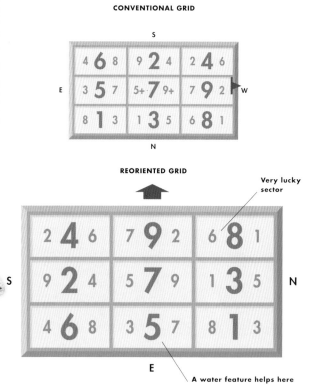

best to have a kitchen here; this will press down on the bad luck. This situation is not so bad during this period of 7 but when the period of 8 comes around it will become a major problem. Place a small water feature here to counter the bad stars combination. It is better if the water is quite close to the back door.

- The southwest sector brings good luck to the matriarch of the house. The 2/6 combination suggests an affluent and easy lifestyle for the matriarch and women of this family. This can be further enhanced by placing metal/gold here to strengthen the 6 star, which is metal.

Main Door Facing West 1

CONVENTIONAL GRID

S

4 **6** 8	9 **2** 4	2 **4** 6
3 **5** 7	5+ **7** 9+	7 **9** 2
8 **1** 3	1 **3** 5	6 **8** 1

E → W

N

REORIENTED GRID

Very lucky sector

2 **4** 6	7 **9** 2	6 **8** 1
9 **2** 4	5 **7** 9	1 **3** 5
4 **6** 8	3 **5** 7	8 **1** 3

S ... N

E

A water feature helps here

AN AFFLUENT LIFESTYLE FOR THE MATRIARCH CAN BE ENCOURAGED BY PLACING METAL – SUCH AS THIS CURVED KNIFE – IN THE SOUTHWEST SECTOR.

WEST 2 OR 3

- In this house the water star of the main door's sector is the lucky number 7 and it also adds up to 10 when combined with the 3 mountain star. This is an auspicious manifestation of the Flying Stars. Hang a seven-rod wind chime near the front door to activate this lucky water star. But please note that the 3/7 combination also indicates armed robbery. This will certainly happen in the period of 8 but can also happen in the present period of 7. Residents should thus be security conscious.

- The back door sector in the east is seriously afflicted. Here the water star is 2 and the main star numeral is 5. The numbers 2 and 5 occurring together cause severe danger to the health of anyone staying in that sector or for the residents if a public area such as the dining or family room is placed here.

- The 2/7 combination also brings bad luck to children, and the 5 main numeral suggests danger related to fire. In addition, during some months of the year when the 2 or 5 is the lo shu of that month, the danger becomes extremely acute. You should position the kitchen or the storeroom in the east, since this contains the bad stars effectively. It is also a very good idea not to have the back door located in that sector. Move it to the northeast or southeast.

- The 2/6 combination in the northeast suggests the prospect of affluence and an easy life that can be enhanced with a wind chime, and the 6/1 combination in the southeast indicates being clever with money.

- The south sector is dangerous. Once again we see the two unlucky numerals of 2 and 5 occurring

together. The water star is afflicted and, this being the sector of fire, anyone staying here could succumb to a fatal illness related to kidneys or sex organs, or they could suffer financial and family loss. You should place a large boulder here to suppress the bad energy. Some suggest using metal.

Main Door Facing West 2 or 3

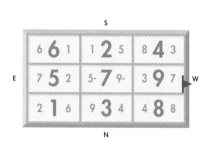

CONVENTIONAL GRID

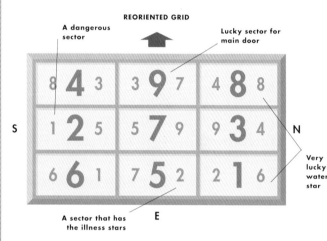

REORIENTED GRID

A dangerous sector

Lucky sector for main door

A sector that has the illness stars

Very lucky water star

PLACE A LARGE BOULDER IN THE SOUTH SECTOR TO SUPPRESS BAD ENERGY. THE SOUTH SECTOR IS DANGEROUS AND COULD BRING MAJOR ILLNESS.

SOUTHWEST 1

- This house enjoys an auspicious front door where it benefits enormously from the double 7 water and mountain stars. The 7 is generally lucky for this period up to 2004. But those with this situation must remember that – come the period of 8 – good luck gets transformed into bad luck and the double 7s then cause armed robbery. So the door needs to be changed before the period of 8. For now, this south-west corner benefits the earth mother. Thus in this house, it is the women and especially the matriarch who benefit most from the auspicious Feng Shui. Anything undertaken by the matriarch is sure to succeed. To ensure this luck is sustained throughout the period, keep the southwest well lit at all times.

- This house suffers from two quarrelsome sectors – west and northwest, with the 3/2 combination. The father or man of the family will be quarrelsome, and when the children grow up they will be argumentative. This is because both the northwest and the west are afflicted. Placing water features – goldfish ponds and aquariums – in these two sectors will help to calm ruffled feathers. Place a quiet water feature or fire with

PLACING A GOLDFISH POND OR AQUARIUM IN THE WEST OR NORTHWEST SECTOR WILL HELP TO PREVENT FAMILY QUARRELS.

metal (red and gold) here to control the bad stars. Those sleeping in these sectors should also ensure their bedrooms stay as quiet as possible.

- The north sector is auspicious. It enjoys the combination of a mountain 6 star and a water 8 star. These two stars bring good fortune to the north. The 6/8 brings wealth and popularity, which can be enhanced with earth or water elements.

- The northeast is also lucky, because it brings popularity and love to residents. It should ideally house the family room or the dining room. Placing plants and a small water feature here would be an excellent idea, but too much water could lead to scandals associated with sex.

- The south and southeast are seriously afflicted. The 5/9 combinations here cause stress and mental afflictions. Use metal to overcome them.

Main Door Facing Southwest 1

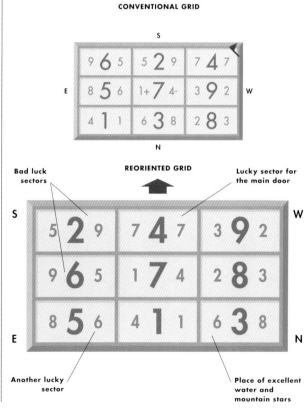

SOUTHWEST 2 OR 3

- This house enjoys a lucky water star in the front door sector. The number 1 is of the water element, so there is no need to build a water feature to enhance the luck. The presence of the number 4, however, indicates an excess of wood element, which in the southwest is not good. This is because wood exhausts and destroys earth. To counter this, place a small metal curved knife in this sector. A metal wind chime is also a good idea. Also, while the 4/1 combination brings romance and social popularity luck, it can also lead to scandals when there is an excess of water.
- The back door area of this house enjoys the precious double 7. If the back door is located in the northeast, therefore, the house will enjoy excellent Feng Shui. But make sure that the kitchen is not also placed here, since this could press down on the good luck of the two 7s.

Upstairs this sector would be ideal as a family area so that everyone benefits from the good Feng Shui.

- The most unlucky room in this house is the east. This is because all three star numerals indicate fatal illness, extreme loss, and even death. The 5 and 2 together is extremely unlucky, and with the 3 thrown in, the whole effect is one of destruction and tears. The combination of 3/2 is also inauspicious and for those in business it leads to law suits. Everything is disharmonious. Place a toilet in this grid area to flush away the bad luck. Some Feng Shui masters recommend placing red and gold paper here to simulate fire and metal (perhaps in wallpaper) to control the 3/2.
- The southeast is also afflicted with the 3/2 combination. Again the use of fire and metal could be effective.
- The south and west have the extremely auspicious 6/8 combination. Bedrooms should be sited here. Enhance with crystals. This combination brings wealth, popularity, prosperity, and authority.

Main Door Facing Southwest 2 or 3

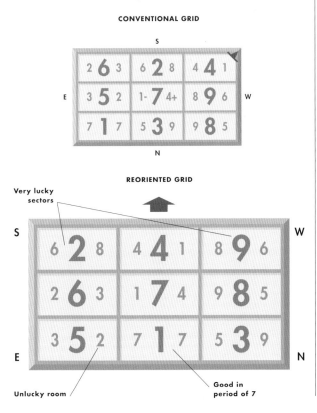

CONVENTIONAL GRID

REORIENTED GRID

Very lucky sectors

Unlucky room

Good in period of 7

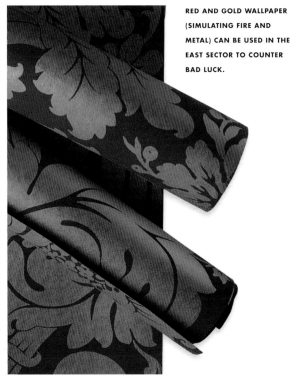

RED AND GOLD WALLPAPER (SIMULATING FIRE AND METAL) CAN BE USED IN THE EAST SECTOR TO COUNTER BAD LUCK.

SOUTHEAST 1

- In this house the front door in the southeast has a lucky water star 7 numeral. But 7 is of the metal element and coming into the corner of wood (the southeast is of the wood element) causes the energies to be in disharmony. Thus, any good luck experienced is soon dissipated and is therefore temporary. The 7/9 combination suggests fire hazards and huge problems caused by overindulgence in sex and flirtations. It is a good idea to use water or earth element objects to control the afflicted stars.

- There is also an unhealthy south grid where the double 2 numerals create the bad luck of loss and illness. The 4/2 combination can also cause problems with in-laws and illnesses associated with the internal organs. Again, use water to overcome this affliction. Do not have a bedroom in the south part of the home.

- The northwest, which is traditionally the place of the patriarch, has an afflicted water star. The 5 star numeral here causes the water star to bring illness to this grid. The 5/7 combination indicates problems associated with the mouth, and this means either mouth-related diseases, danger of poisoning, or problems caused by excessive chatter. Use water to overcome this affliction.

- The north sector has an excellent 3/1 combination, which suggests wealth and popularity, but this sector will also benefit from the presence of water because the north is of the water element. To have a lucky water star here, and with the number 1 being water as well, good fortune comes easily. Do not overdo things, however, and stay balanced.

- The sector to avoid using is the northeast, where the 5/3 combination is extremely bad for wealth. It is worse here because the 5 is the mountain star. Do not have your bedroom here and do not energize anything here. Place the toilet or storeroom in this part of the house.

FIRE HAZARDS ARE A FEATURE IN THE SOUTHEAST SECTOR. USE WATER OR EARTH ELEMENT OBJECTS IN THIS SECTOR TO CONTROL THE AFFLICTED STARS.

Main Door Facing Southeast 1

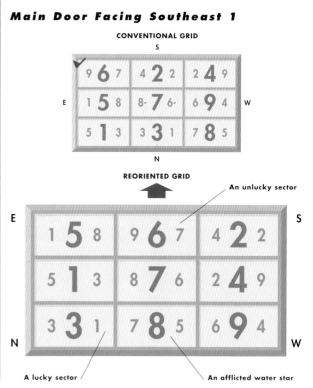

SOUTHEAST 2 OR 3

- This house has an afflicted water star numeral 5 in the front door grid in the southeast. All the residents will suffer because of this. Try to find another door because this is a feature that brings bad luck to the house. The combination of 5/7 indicates problems concerning gossip and bad reputation. It also causes illness relating to the mouth. The bad luck is experienced in both periods of 7 and 8. Placing a large green plant near the front door will dissolve the bad luck but not completely. The mountain star of 7 is auspicious, so some boulders will be good. Some masters recommend using water, while others suggest metal (such as a wind chime) to overcome the bad stars.
- The house is afflicted by the 3/2 combination in south and north. The 3/1 combination in the south suggests wealth and popularity, while the 4/2 of the north indicates health problems related to the internal organs. Counter this affliction in the north by putting an urn filled with water here. This cools down fiery tempers and overcomes the health problems to some extent. In the south, activate the wealth aspects of the good combination stars with water. This energizes the auspicious 1 water star while simultaneously calming tempers caused by the 3/2 quarrelsome stars.

AN URN FILLED WITH WATER IN THE NORTH SECTOR WILL HELP TO COOL DOWN FIERY TEMPERS AND OVERCOME HEALTH PROBLEMS.

- The 4/6 of the east indicates inauspicious luck for the women of the household who will tend to suffer indignities. There is no specific cure. Women should not sleep in this area of the house.
- The 2/9 of the northeast indicates sluggishness and simplemindedness. This is not good for college students, since this hurts their grades even though the north east generally brings good education luck.
- The 5/3 of the southwest is bad for wealth luck. It causes loss and plenty of money problems. Do not have a bedroom here. One good cure is metal, which weakens the earth element.
- The northwest has the combination of 9/7, which usually means that the men in the family tend to be "playboys" and have roving eyes. They cause no end of heartaches for their spouses. To overcome this, place an urn filled with still water here.

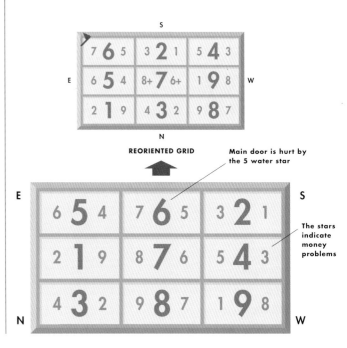

PLACING GREEN PLANTS NEAR THE ENTRANCE HELPS TO ALLEVIATE THE BAD LUCK STARS OF THE SECTOR, BUT NOT COMPLETELY.

Main Door Facing Southeast 2 or 3

CONVENTIONAL GRID

S

7 6 5	3 2 1	5 4 3
6 5 4	8+ 7 6+	1 9 8
2 1 9	4 3 2	9 8 7

E ... W

N

REORIENTED GRID

Main door is hurt by the 5 water star

E	6 5 4	7 6 5	3 2 1	S
	2 1 9	8 7 6	5 4 3	
N	4 3 2	9 8 7	1 9 8	W

The stars indicate money problems

NORTHEAST 1

- This house has the 1/4 combination in the northeast where the main door is, indicating scholarly achievements, media attention, publicity, and romance. The water star 4 represents wood in the mountain. This is not so good but the mountain star 1 strengthens the earth element of the northeast, thereby bringing good luck, so the main door is not badly afflicted.

Main Door Facing Northeast 1

CONVENTIONAL GRID

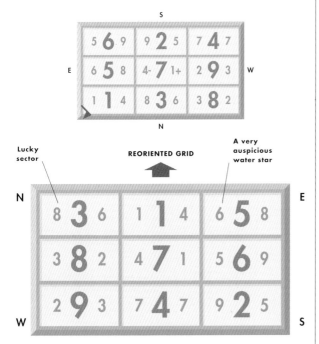

REORIENTED GRID

Lucky sector

A very auspicious water star

MEDIA ATTENTION OR OTHER PUBLICITY, TOGETHER WITH ROMANCE, MAY COME TO THOSE WHOSE FRONT DOOR IS IN NORTHEAST 1.

- The back door in the southwest has the auspicious double 7 combination of water and mountain stars, indicating luck coming when least expected – like gold being discovered in the mountain – a good sign. Place a bedroom here. Do not place the kitchen here. The double 7 is lucky only in the period of 7. When the time cycle changes to the period of 8 it becomes dangerous and indicates armed robbery. So either

change the natal chart altogether or remedy the situation after 2004 by pressing down the 7s with the fire element. This means bright lights kept turned on through the night.

- The southeast and south sectors are afflicted with the 5/9 and 9/5 combinations. These are bad luck, stress, pressure, and illness stars. There is no consensus among master practitioners of Flying Star Feng Shui on how to overcome these combinations. Some suggest using sturdy plants to control the earth of 5 while enhancing the fire of 9. Others suggest metal to exhaust the earth of 5 and aggravate the fire of 9. I advise not to sleep in these two sectors if possible, and to place a storeroom here.

- The northwest and west have the quarrelsome 3/2 and 2/3 combinations. Using red and gold will help to alleviate the bad Chi of these sectors.

- The north and the east benefit from the 8/6 and 6/8 combinations, which bring wealth and prosperity. But the east has the main numeral 5, which causes obstacles to wealth, and the north has the main star numeral of 3, which is also not auspicious. To enjoy good luck, therefore, strengthen the water and mountain stars with element enhancers to get the best of the good combinations.

NORTHEAST 2 OR 3

- This house has the auspicious double 7 combination of water and mountain stars in the northeast where the main door is located – an excellent combination that spells wealth and success luck for this period of 7. When the time cycle changes to 8 it indicates armed robbery, so change the door direction before 2004.

- The back door in the southwest has the 1/4 combination. This is excellent and can be enhanced with a high fence at the back to tap the auspicious mountain star.

- The northwest and north sectors are afflicted with the 5/9 and 9/5 combinations. These are bad luck, stress, pressure, and illness stars. Hong Kong masters suggest using wood element to control the 5 earth while enhancing the 9 fire. Other practitioners use metal to exhaust the 5 earth and aggravate the 9 fire.

- The southeast and east have the quarrelsome 3/2 and 2/3 combinations. Using red and gold will help to alleviate the bad chi of these sectors.

- The south and the west benefit from the 8/6 and 6/8 combinations, which bring wealth and prosperity, so the back of the house is luckier than the front in terms of locations for bedrooms.

- The auspicious 1/4 in the southwest brings fame and recognition to the women of the household. On no account should water be placed in this sector, since water spoils everything and will turn fame into notoriety and recognition into scandal.

A HIGH BACKYARD FENCE OR WALL WILL ENHANCE GOOD LUCK WHEN THE BACK DOOR IS IN THE SOUTHWEST.

Main Door Facing Northeast 2 or 3

CONVENTIONAL GRID

S

3 **6** 2	8 **2** 6	1 **4** 4
2 **5** 3	4+ **7** 1-	6 **9** 8
7 **1** 7	9 **3** 5	5 **8** 9

E — W

N

REORIENTED GRID

Unlucky sectors

Sectors with quarrelsome stars

N — E

9 **3** 5	7 **1** 7	2 **5** 3
5 **8** 9	4 **7** 1	3 **6** 2
6 **9** 8	1 **4** 4	8 **2** 6

W — S

Lucky sector

NORTHWEST 1

- The main door of this house has the lucky 7 numeral for the water star and the unlucky 5 numeral for the mountain star. This is the northwest sector, which has metal as its element, so the 7 star enhances this metal and therefore creates good harmony. The 5 star is of the earth element, which produces metal. On balance, therefore, the main door is absolutely fine in this period of 7. However, the 5/7 combination is a negative one and in the next period residents will suffer from gossip and loss of reputation.

THE MAIN DOOR OF THIS HOUSE HAS A LUCKY 7 FOR THE WATER STAR AND AN UNLUCKY 5 FOR THE MOUNTAIN STAR.

- The south sector suffers from the presence of the double 2 star numerals and the 2/4 combination, which indicates marriage and in-law problems. It is best not to have the master bedroom here.
- The 2/9 of the southwest spells bad luck for children's education. Avoid bedrooms for them in this part of the house.
- The northeast has the unlucky 3/5 combination, which means loss of wealth and cash flow problems aplenty. Overcome this with metal, although this will probably only be partly successful. It is best to have a storeroom here to capture the bad stars. Do not work or sleep here.
- The 4/6 combination in the west grid indicates it is most unsuitable for the daughters of the family. You should place sons here instead, if you have sons.
- The center of the house is the most auspicious sector because it has the 8/6 combination of water and mountain stars. It is a good idea to place the master bedroom in the center of the house.

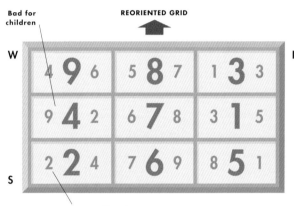

CONVENTIONAL GRID

REORIENTED GRID

Bad for children

Very afflicted – anyone staying here will get very sick

A CHILD'S EDUCATION COULD BE ADVERSELY AFFECTED IF HIS OR HER BEDROOM IS LOCATED IN THE SOUTHWEST SECTOR OF A HOUSE WHOSE MAIN DOOR IS LOCATED IN THE NORTHWEST 1 SUBDIRECTION.

NORTHWEST 2 OR 3

- The main door of this house has three lucky numerals: 9 for the water star, 7 for the mountain star, and 8 for the main star numeral. This indicates continued prosperity for the family – present, future, and distant prosperity are all indicated. This generally means good fortune for the descendants as well. The good fortune will be better in the next period than in this present period. The 7/9 combination, however, indicates that the men of the family tend to have roving eyes and have affairs outside the marriage.
- This house suffers from two bad corners, which are afflicted by the 2/3 quarrelsome combination. In the north the mountain star 2 combines with the main numeral star 3 to indicate a great deal of arguments and misunderstandings. Place a big urn filled with water to cope with these two stars. The 2/4 combinations indicates severe marriage problems.

IN HOUSES WHERE THE MAIN DOOR IS IN THE NORTHWEST 2 OR 3 SUBDIRECTIONS MEN OF THE FAMILY TEND TO HAVE ROVING EYES AND TO HAVE AFFAIRS OUTSIDE THE MARRIAGE.

Main Door Facing Northwest 2 or 3

CONVENTIONAL GRID

S

E			W
	5 6 7	1 2 3	3 4 5
	4 5 6	6+ 7 8+	8 9 1
	9 1 2	2 3 4	7 8 9

N

REORIENTED GRID

Excellent sector for the main door

Inauspicious sectors

W			N
8 9 1	7 8 9	2 3 4	
3 4 5	6 7 8	9 1 2	
1 2 3	5 6 7	4 5 6	
S			E

- In the south the water star numeral is 3, and this number is of the wood element. This feeds the fire of this sector, causing grievous problems and even violence because of the 3/2 combination. In this sector the 3/2 configuration is much more serious than in the north sector. Place a very large presence of water here to cool down the fire. The 1/3 combination – which usually means wealth – is in this case afflicted. It indicates someone leaving home instead. The use of objects associated with the element of water alleviates this problem.

WATCHPOINT

Place a big urn filled with water in the north to counteract bad luck.

- The northeast corner is also afflicted with the 2/9 combination. This brings bad luck for studies and education, so do not energize the northeast for your college students or schoolchildren.

Finetuning the Flying Stars

Developing knowledge of the Flying Star Formula requires patience. This is an area of Feng Shui that requires serious study before understanding is adequate, but perseverance and the quest for knowledge will help those who are really keen. There are two areas where I can pass on additional information – combining Flying Stars with color, and exploring the reigning numbers of months, weeks, and days. If you want to take it further, I refer you to advanced text of Flying Star Feng Shui.

COLORS IN FLYING STAR FENG SHUI

A supplementary text on Flying Star Feng Shui assigns colors to each of the nine numbers and then goes on to identify the auspicious and inauspicious color numbers. The most auspicious numerals are the white  numerals, which are 1, 6, and 8. These are known as the white stars and their presence in any sector brings intangible forces, that in turn bring excellent good fortune. The white stars enhance good Landscape Feng Shui. They are also effective in modifying and killing the bad effects caused by other inauspicious Feng Shui features or numbers.

The white stars are collectively known as the triple stars. When they occur together in the sector where the main door is located, this spells enormous good fortune during an entire twenty-year period.

The killing numerals are the black and yellow numerals. The black numeral is 2, while the yellow numeral is 5. When black combines with yellow it creates extreme ill fortune. Therefore, when 2 and 5 occur together, it is a warning of impending bad luck.

Other color numerals are as follows:

- The number 3 is pure green, and the number 4 is light green. These numerals are neither good nor bad, but when 3 is combined with 2, hostility and anger are created.
- The number 7 is maroon or brown. This numeral is auspicious during the current period. In the period of 8, the numeral 7 loses its auspicious effect.
- The number 9 is purple, which is very good fortune, although it takes a long time for the good fortune to manifest.

YEARLY, MONTHLY, AND WEEKLY LO SHU GRIDS

Flying Star Feng Shui is divinitive in that it has a significant time dimension to its practice. This requires you to have the hundred-year Hsia calendar, which gives you the Lo Shu squares for each year, month, and week. By matching those numbers with the numbers of the Flying Stars of your home or office, you will be able to predict with remarkable accuracy when you could get

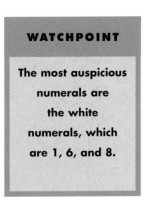

WATCHPOINT
The most auspicious numerals are the white numerals, which are 1, 6, and 8.

robbed, when you will have losses, when certain rooms will cause death, accidents, or severe illness, and so forth. Needless to say, the divinitive side of Flying Star Feng Shui is not included in this book, because it is simply beyond its scope, requiring far more advanced study into the casting of the natal charts and also understanding the Chinese calendar in greater depth.

Those interested in exploring Feng Shui more deeply are strongly advised to learn how to read the Chinese calendar first and how to extract the Lo Shu reigning numbers of months, weeks, days, and hours from it. After that, seek out a genuine and authentic master who is well skilled in this particular

method of Feng Shui. It will take 12 to 18 months to become really competent in the practice of the complete Flying Star Formula. Another point to remember is that genuine Feng Shui masters rarely impart their full secrets immediately. You have to win their trust. To do this stay humble at all times.

For initial explorations into Flying Star Feng Shui, the Lo Shu numbers for the next hundred years are adequate. Remember that the numbers in the nine different sectors must be analyzed in conjunction with the natal chart of the home so that you can examine the combination of the numbers in any sector at any moment.

REIGNING LO SHU NUMBER IN CENTER OF LO SHU GRID (SEE PAGE 61)	THE REIGNING NUMBER APPLIES TO THESE YEARS IN THE HUNDRED-YEAR CHINESE OR LUNAR CALENDAR
1	2008, 2017, 2026, 2035. 2044, 2053, 2062, 2071, 2080, and 2089
2	2007, 2016, 2025, 2034, 2043, 2052, 2061, 2070, 2079, 2088, and 2097
3	2006, 2015, 2024, 2033, 2042, 2051, 2060, 2069, 2078, 2087, and 2096
4	2005, 2014, 2023, 2032, 2041, 2050, 2059, 2068, 2077, 2086, and 2095
5	2004, 2013, 2022, 2031, 2040, 2049, 2058, 2067, 2076, 2085, and 2094
6	2003, 2012, 2021, 2030, 2039, 2048, 2057, 2066, 2075, 2084, and 2093
7	2002, 2011, 2020, 2029, 2038, 2047, 2056, 2065, 2074, 2083, and 2092
8	2001, 2010, 2019, 2028, 2037, 2046, 2055, 2064, 2073, 2082, and 2091
9	2000, 2009, 2018, 2027, 2036, 2045, 2054, 2063, 2072, 2081, and 2090

5

TIME TABOOS FOR RENOVATIONS

This chapter is concerned with taking your knowledge of Flying Star Feng Shui one step further. Just as there are good and bad sectors in the home, depending on the direction in which your main door faces and the age of the building in which you live, so there are three specific locations that are best not disturbed by renovation or redecoration. These are known as the Grand Duke Jupiter, the Three Killings, and the Five Yellow – and their positions alter each year. Provided here are details for each of these three directions and tips on how to establish where they are and how best to avoid their negative influences.

Annual Inauspicious Sectors

Taking a time perspective on luck is a vital part of Feng Shui practice. Thus, although you may have had your home, shop, or office splendidly decked out according to solid Feng Shui guidelines, you should never forget to periodically check on the Feng Shui effect of time, which requires knowledge of the Flying Star Formula. Flying Star Feng Shui focuses on intangible forces that can play havoc with Chi flows. In this chapter we look at time taboos on home renovations and redecoration.

If you are thinking of extending your home, doing some repainting, or have plans to renovate, you are strongly advised to observe certain restrictions regarding the timing and location of the renovation. Otherwise, you could suffer bad luck throughout the year, and sometimes even for a period of anything from two to twenty years. So, before you undertake any kind of construction work inside or on your building, be aware of three important sectors in your home, office, or shop. These are colorfully named as the Grand Duke Jupiter, the Three Killings, and the Five Yellow.

THE GRAND DUKE JUPITER

The Grand Duke (known as *tai sui* in Chinese) changes location every year, and it is vital that you find out where he resides each year because you must never incur the wrath of the Grand Duke by confronting him. In Feng Shui terms, confrontation occurs when you disturb the particular location indicated, or when you sit facing him.

If you confront the Grand Duke you are certain to suffer defeat, demotion, and severe loss. Should you be involved in a combative or competitive situation with

> **WATCHPOINT**
>
> **You should never face the Grand Duke, even if that is your best direction.**

anyone in the year, you will lose if you inadvertently offend the Grand Duke. It is for this reason that the first thing Feng Shui masters in Hong Kong do each new year is to calculate the Grand Duke's location and identify it for their clients.

Please note that the Grand Duke occupies only 15 degrees of the compass. Thus it is quite easy to avoid offending him; the rules to observe are as follows:

Rule 1: You should never sit in a position that is directly opposite to the Grand Duke. For example in 2005, the year of the Rooster, the Grand Duke is in the west sector of your home. So do not sit facing this direction. No matter how auspicious facing west is for you under the Eight Mansions Formula, strenuously guard against doing this.

The strength of the Grand Duke is such that even if he is located in your best direction, you must be sure not to sit facing him. So during the year of the Rooster, for example, West Group people should not face the west, even if this is their most auspicious direction. It is never worth confronting the Grand Duke because you will lose out every time. Consult the table opposite to check the Grand Duke's location for the next ten years. If you do not observe this rule in

Feng Shui, you may be confronting the Grand Duke and not even know it.

Rule 2: Never disturb the Grand Duke, or you might incur his wrath. This means that in 2003, for example, you should not undertake any renovation or construction works in the south-southwest. If you are planning to make changes that involve construction work then always be sure to first determine the sector of your home in which the Grand Duke is located for any particular year. Use a good compass to determine this sector (superimpose the nine-sector Lo Shu grid to help you demarcate it). If in doubt, it is better to postpone your plans! This rule is equally applicable for land or buildings. If you break this taboo, Feng Shui masters warn of grave misfortune. Ancient Chinese warlords always avoided advancing into battle in the direction of the Grand Duke. They always made sure the Grand Duke was behind them, and therefore supporting them.

One interesting fact to note is that during the Gulf War in 1991, when Saddam Hussein's forces were pitted against the Allied Forces of the West, the Grand Duke was in the southwest. The allies were headquartered in Saudi Arabia and when advancing toward Kuwait they had southwest behind them, thus having the Grand Duke behind them. Saddam's forces, on the other hand, advanced to the southwest, thereby directly confronting the Grand Duke. Accordingly, the Feng Shui of the Allied Forces was superior to that of Saddam's forces.

THE LOCATIONS OF THE GRAND DUKE

The Grand Duke's locations during each of the ten animal years of the lunar calendar from 2000 until 2009 are summarized in the table to the right. Please refer to the hundred-year calendar on pages 32–33 for the exact start and end of each lunar New Year.

BEFORE REDECORATING YOUR HOME YOU ARE STRONGLY ADVISED TO OBSERVE CERTAIN RESTRICTIONS REGARDING TIMING AND LOCATION.

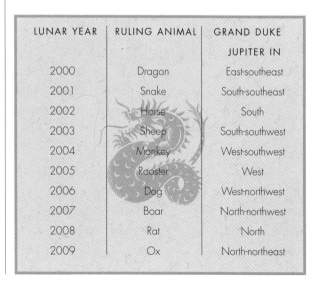

LUNAR YEAR	RULING ANIMAL	GRAND DUKE JUPITER IN
2000	Dragon	East-southeast
2001	Snake	South-southeast
2002	Horse	South
2003	Sheep	South-southwest
2004	Monkey	West-southwest
2005	Rooster	West
2006	Dog	West-northwest
2007	Boar	North-northwest
2008	Rat	North
2009	Ox	North-northeast

THE THREE KILLINGS

In Cantonese, this location is known as *sarm sart*, meaning Three Killings! It is the location that conflicts directly with that of the Grand Duke. It is also a location that must be confronted. You cannot have the Three Killings behind you. Instead, you must face it directly. Home repairs and renovations may be undertaken in locations opposite the Three Killings but not in locations housing the Three Killings. When you directly confront the Three Killings you can overcome it, but if you disturb it in its own domain, you are seriously asking for trouble!

It is easy to work out the location of the Three Killings for any given year as it occupies 90 degrees of the compass. Once you have checked in which animal year you are planning renovations you can determine where the Three Killings is located using the chart above. For example, in the year of the Dragon it will be in the south, so be sure not to undertake major repairs in the south sector of your home that year.

Here are two useful rules to follow regarding the Three Killings:

Rule 1: You must never have the Three Killings behind you in any year. Instead, you should face it and confront it. Thus when it is in the west, you should sit facing the west. You should not have the west behind you. In the year 2004 you should sit north facing south rather than vice versa.

Rule 2: Home repairs and renovations may be undertaken in locations opposite the Three Killings but not in locations housing the Three Killings. According to the texts if you so much as dig a single hole in the ground where the Three Killings is located, or cut down a tree there, you will be attacked by three types of

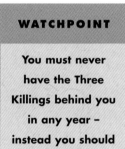

WATCHPOINT

You must never have the Three Killings behind you in any year – instead you should confront it.

HOME RENOVATION, WHICH CAN INCLUDE REDECORATION, MAY BE UNDERTAKEN IN LOCATIONS OPPOSITE THE THREE KILLINGS, BUT NOT IN LOCATIONS HOUSING THE THREE KILLINGS. *SEE* CHART ABOVE.

LOCATIONS OF THE THREE KILLINGS	
DURING ANIMAL YEAR	THREE KILLINGS IS IN THE
Ox, rooster, and snake	east
Boar, rabbit, and sheep	west
Monkey, rat, and dragon	south
Dog, horse, and tiger	north

misfortunes – so do be very careful when undertaking renovations in these locations.

THE FIVE YELLOW

A third configuration of negative intangible forces is expressed as the Five Yellow (*wu wang* in Chinese). This is when the extremely inauspicious yellow star numeral 5 enters a particular sector under the yearly Lo Shu grid. All renovation work in the sector containing the Five Yellow will create severe problems for the household. It is also an excellent idea to hang a six-rod wind chime to press

HANG A SIX-ROD WIND CHIME TO PRESS DOWN ON THE BAD LUCK OF THE FIVE YELLOW IN THE SECTOR WHERE IT APPEARS.

down on the bad luck of the Five Yellow in the sector where it appears. The location of the Five Yellow for the next ten years is presented in the table.

The Five Yellow is particularly distressing because even when you do not disturb it, it brings misfortunes. Thus in the year 2001, for example, you should leave the southwest well alone.

This star brings severe illness, loss, and grave misfortunes. It occupies 45 degrees of the compass (360 degrees divided by 8 = 45) and you should avoid digging, cutting, or banging in the sector in which it resides. If you find your main door is located in that sector for a particular year then hang a wind chime to press down on the Five Yellow. Another good method is to display the laughing Buddha in that sector.

LOCATIONS OF THE FIVE YELLOW

IN THE FOLLOWING LUNAR YEARS	FIVE YELLOW IS LOCATED IN THE
2000	north
2001	southwest
2002	east
2003	southeast
2004	center
2005	northwest
2006	west
2007	northeast
2008	south
2009	north

SOUTH

8	4	6
7	9	2
3	5	1

NORTH

THE ANNUAL LO SHU CHART FOR 2000 SHOWS THE FIVE YELLOW IN THE NORTH SECTOR: IT IS PARTICULARLY DISTRESSING BECAUSE IT BRINGS MISFORTUNE EVEN WHEN YOU DO NOT DISTURB IT.

6

REDECORATING FOR AUSPICIOUS LUCK

The Lo Shu grid is central to so much that is potent in Feng Shui. Each of the formulas explained so far in this book makes use of its invaluable pattern of numbers, and this chapter is no exception. Armed with the relevant Lo Shu grid for the year of your decoration and a knowledge of the auspicious numbers (1, 6, 7, and 8) you can set about introducing plenty of Yang energy to the most important places of your home. This is further enhanced with the use of color, which is closely related to the different sectors of the Lo Shu grid. The following pages provide you with options for making your best choices.

Selecting Auspicious Sectors

f you want to use Feng Shui to jump-start your good fortune, one excellent method is to introduce a massive dose of precious sheng chi and Yang energy into specific corners in the home. Arrange to redecorate these areas in your home to create auspicious new energy. Bring in new furnishings, decorations, carpets, and flooring – or apply a fresh coat of paint.

This technique of attracting good sheng chi into the home has to be planned according to the Lo Shu grid. When you look at the Lo Shu grid that represents each year (*see* pages 61 and 89) you will be able to pinpoint the specific part of your home that will benefit from an injection of new energy brought about by redecoration or extension works. The key to success is to select the correct sector or room(s) to redecorate in any particular year.

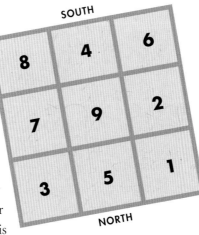

SOUTH

8	4	6
7	9	2
3	5	1

NORTH

THIS LO SHU GRID IS RELEVANT FOR YEARS IN WHICH THE REIGNING NUMBER IS 9. THE YEAR 2000 HAS THIS GRID WITH THE 9 IN THE CENTER.

NEW DECORATIONS, SUCH AS WALLPAPER, CAN HELP INJECT FRESH POSITIVE ENERGY INTO YOUR HOME IF YOU ARE CAREFUL TO DECORATE IN AN AUSPICIOUS YEAR.

1 *Using the table on page 89 and Lo Shu grids on page 61, establish the relevant grid for the year you plan on doing the redecoration. For instance, if you plan to redecorate in the lunar year 2000 then the reigning number for that year is 9, and the relevant Lo Shu square will have 9 in the center of the grid (see diagram of grid above).*

2 *Check the lunar calendar on pages 32–33 to make sure you get the dates correct.*

3 *Now you can superimpose the relevant Lo Shu square onto your floor plan.*

4 *Next refer to Chapter 5 and check the corners where you must NOT undertake any renovation during the year 2000. This means checking where the locations of the Grand Duke Jupiter, the Three Killings, and the Five Yellow are. Remember that this investigation is to determine which sectors are taboo for renovation. Simple redecoration is allowed. It is only when your redecoration involves digging and cutting that it is considered taboo. In the year 2000, the Grand Duke is in the east-southeast, Three Killings is in the west, and the Five Yellow is in the north.*

5 *Next, check which sectors of your home have the numerals of 1, 6, 7, and 8. These are the auspicious numbers and their location indicates the lucky sectors during that particular year. Thus in the year 2000, which has 9 as the reigning number, the location of the auspicious numbers are 1 – the northwest; 6 – the southwest; 7 – the east; 8 – the southeast.*

In the year 2000, then, if the rooms in the home that are located in the northwest (1) and southwest (6) are redecorated or renovated, good fortune is energized for the entire home.

Furthermore, if these two directions also represent your auspicious directions (in this case, if you are a West Group person) the result is doubly auspicious for you, since you will be generating a good amount of

REDECORATION WILL BRING GOOD FORTUNE TO A HOUSEHOLD IF IT IS CARRIED OUT IN ACCORDANCE WITH GOOD FLYING STAR CONSIDERATIONS AND TABOOS.

fresh new energy into your own direction. If these directions do not happen to be good for you, then redecoration of the home will still bring good fortune for the household.

> **WATCHPOINT**
>
> **Redecorate the rooms that correspond with the good luck numbers 1, 6, 7, and 8.**

Renovating for Immediate Luck

To renovate for immediate prosperity luck during this period of 7, which ends in the year 2004, you should look out for the year between now and 2004 when you can profitably energize the number 7. This number represents immediate prosperity because 7 is the lucky number for this period. The table opposite summarizes the location of the number 7 up to the year 2004. It also includes the place of the Grand Duke in each year so that you can tell if it is possible to energize 7 that year by having a redecoration project in the 7 sector.

After the year 2004 and for the next twenty-year period, the number that represents immediate prosperity is the lucky white number 8. Energizing sector 8 will bring tremendous good fortune if you get the year correct. During the period of 8 the number 7 is no longer lucky. But during the period of 7, the number 8 is still regarded as being lucky.

The table opposite summarizes what you can and cannot do from 2000 through to 2009. There is a cutoff point in year 2004 to allow for the changeover from the period of 7 to the period of 8. In the right-hand column I have offered suggestions on color schemes. These are based primarily on the energizing of the dominant element of the particular compass sector being activated.

You can take your cue from here and decorate with objects that suggest these same elements or use elements that are considered to be productive in the cycle of elements (*see* pages 118–119).

DECORATING YOUR HOUSE WITH LUSH, GREEN PLANTS AND WOODEN OBJECTS WILL PROMOTE GOOD FORTUNE BUT ALWAYS NOTE THE LOCATION OF THE GRAND DUKE.

LUNAR YEAR	LOCATION OF 7 IN LO SHU GRID	LOCATION OF GRAND DUKE	FENG SHUI ADVICE ON RENOVATION AND REDECORATION FOR IMMEDIATE PROSPERITY IN THE 7/8 SECTORS
2000	east	east-southeast	Do not do anything to the 7 sector east since the Grand Duke is there this year.
2001	southeast	south-southeast	Do not do anything to the 7 sector southeast since you could inadvertently be confronting the Grand Duke.
2002	center	south	Redecorate the center of your home this year (perhaps the family room). Use combinations of red and yellow.
2003	northwest	south-southwest	Redecorate or renovate the northwest this year. Use metallic colors or shades of white.
	LOCATION OF 8 IN LO SHU GRID		
2004	northeast	west-southwest	Redecorate the northeast 8 sector. Use combinations of earth colors to create auspicious Chi energy.
2005	south	west	Yes, you can redecorate the south in shades of red. An excellent year to bring in precious Yang energies.
2006	north	west-northwest	This is an excellent year to activate water in the north sector for immediate prosperity luck. Use shades of blue and black in your choice of soft furnishings.
2007	southwest	north-northwest	Energize the southwest with new wallpaper, carpets, and drapes. Build additions if you wish. Use earth tones and colors.
2008	east	north	Activate for immediate prosperity by using shades of wood colors for the east sector – greens or browns. For the east I always prefer greens because this denotes growth and development.
2009	southeast	north-northeast	Another good year for energizing the southeast with wood element energy. Once again use shades of green to create an effective wealth corner.

Renovating for Long-term Luck

Long-term prosperity is in many ways even more important than immediate prosperity. Long-term prosperity suggests a continuance of good fortune. The Chinese regard long term as being better than short term, and good fortune is defined as one's life getting better and better, that one's prosperity grows with age.

To activate long-term prosperity luck during this period of 7 you should note the location of the numeral 8 on the Lo Shu square up to the year 2004. When the period of 7 changes to the period of 8, from the year 2004, it is the sector of the Lo Shu that contains the numeral 9 that has to be activated.

Both 8 and 9 are auspicious numbers, and in Flying Star Feng Shui the number 8 is regarded as being extremely auspicious. The number 9, however, is considered to be the ultimate numeral since it represents the fullness of heaven and earth. There is no higher number than nine, and nine multiplied by itself to infinity continues to be nine. Thus, 9 x 9 = 81 and 8 + 1 = 9. Try this with 9 times anything and still you will come back to nine.

As with the exercise of energizing immediate prosperity luck, you should always check where the Grand Duke direction is in the year you are making renovations to your home. This is to make sure you do not inadvertently confront the Grand Duke.

The table opposite summarizes advice for long-term prosperity from 2000 to 2009. In the year 2004, allow for the changeover from period of 7 to 8.

LOCATIONS OF NUMBERS 6 AND 1		
LUNAR YEAR	LOCATION OF 6 IN LO SHU GRID	LOCATION OF 1 IN LO SHU GRID
2000	southwest	northwest
2001	east	west
2002	southeast	northeast
2003	center	south
2004	northwest (exceptionally auspicious year to redecorate this location)	north (exceptionally auspicious year to redecorate this location)
2005	west	southwest
2006	northeast	east
2007	south	southeast
2008	north	center
2009	southwest	northwest

SIX BLESSINGS FROM HEAVEN

The Six Blessings from Heaven is indicated by 6 in the Lo Shu grid. In Flying Star Feng Shui, 6 is especially potent in bringing good fortune when it falls in the northwest since this symbolizes heaven. The trigram Chien is placed here and 6 is also the number of the northwest. In the next ten years, 6 falls in the northwest in 2004 and reappears in 2013 and 2022. In these lunar years the northwest should be strongly energized.

Change the energy of the home by renovating the northwest during these years and attract six major blessings from heaven – wealth, health, descendants, fame, patronage, and power, by using the Nine Aspirations Formula (*see* pages 48–55). Bring gold (e.g., gold-painted rocks) and metal into the northwest because this section is ruled by the element of metal.

THE MAGIC OF ONE

This refers to the location where 1 is in the Lo Shu grid. Like 6, 1 is regarded as an auspicious white-colored number. Locations that enjoy the presence of this numeral will enjoy good luck (*see* table opposite).

LUNAR YEAR	LOCATION OF 8 IN LO SHU GRID	LOCATION OF GRAND DUKE	FENG SHUI ADVICE ON RENOVATION AND REDECORATION FOR LONG-TERM PROSPERITY IN THE 8/9 SECTOR
2000	southeast	east-southeast	Do not do anything in the southeast this year.
2001	center	south-southeast	You can redecorate and renovate the center part of your home to activate long-term prosperity.
2002	northwest	south	Energize the northwest with textures of white and off-white shades. Hang six- or eight-rod wind chimes here.
2003	west	south-southwest	Energize the west with metallic color schemes and also hang an eight–rod wind chime here.
LOCATION OF 9 IN LO SHU GRID			
2004	south	west-southwest	Exceptionally good year to renovate the south. Use new lights to create a new look, and adopt a bright yellow or red color scheme.
2005	north	west	Activate the water element in the north. Use blues and blacks.
2006	southwest	west-northwest	Energize the southwest with ocher and other earth colors. Decorate with ceramics and crystals.
2007	east	north-northwest	Use plants to energize the east if your living room is here. In bedrooms, use green color schemes.
2008	southeast	north	If the southeast is your living or dining room, use plants. Or use greens to create a new look.
2009	center	north-northeast	You can redecorate and renovate the center part of your home to activate long-term prosperity.

7

THE FOUR PILLARS FORMULA

The Four Pillars relate specifically to the hour, day, month, and year of your birth. Know these and you can cast a natal chart that describes the basket of elements which affect you personally. Focus on the year and hour pillars to discover your mix of Yin and Yang energies. This information also allows you to balance the energies in your home, providing you with as favorable an outlook on life as is possible. You can also energize the area of your home associated with your ruling animal in the Chinese astrological calendar.

The Four Pillars of Destiny

The Four Pillars of Destiny refer to the hour, the day, the month, and the year of your birth. Based on these four pieces of information, Chinese astrology can cast a natal chart from which a detailed reading of the ups and downs of your life can be charted. This is what Chinese fortunetellers claim they can do.

Chinese astrology has little to do with the sun, moon, and stars directly. Unlike Western or Indian astrology, it does not look heavenward to chart the movement of constellations either to draw up a personality composite of an individual or to predict that person's destiny. Rather, Chinese astrology uses specific calendar dates, times, and tables to figure out the dominant five elements in anyone's Four Pillars chart.

YOUR EIGHT CHARACTERS AND THEIR SIGNIFICANCE

If you know your Four Pillars, i.e., if you know exactly your time, day, month, and year of birth, as well as the place of your birth, you will be able to use the Chinese hundred-year calendar to figure out your Eight Characters. These Eight Characters refer to the element equivalents of each of the pillars. Thus, for the year of birth there is an element

that represents the heavenly stem and an element that represents the earthly branch of that year. These are the two characters of the year pillar. Similarly, there are two characters of the month, day, and hour pillars, making a total of Eight Characters.

Discovering the complete Eight Characters requires a great deal of checking, counterchecking, referencing and

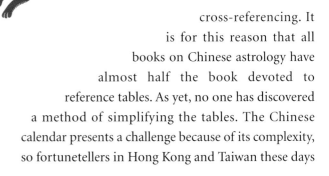

cross-referencing. It is for this reason that all books on Chinese astrology have almost half the book devoted to reference tables. As yet, no one has discovered a method of simplifying the tables. The Chinese calendar presents a challenge because of its complexity, so fortunetellers in Hong Kong and Taiwan these days resort to the computer to figure out a full chart for their clients, thereby overcoming the tedious task of manual computations.

The most difficult part of the astrology computation is obtaining the two characters of the day pillar. However, for Feng Shui purposes, the effect of the day pillar is relatively insignificant. In view of this, I usually ignore the day pillar whenever I use the Four Pillars method to diagnose Feng Shui. Instead, I concentrate on analyzing the year and hour pillars, since these are the most important pillars that have a bearing on the personalized Feng Shui of any home.

HEAVENLY STEMS AND EARTHLY BRANCHES

The Chinese calendar is made up of sixty-year cycles that are differentiated according to heavenly stems and earthly branches. There are 10 stems and 12 branches in total. In the sixty-year cycle the stems comprise the five elements, each in a Yin and Yang aspect, while the branches are the 12 animals of the Chinese Zodiac. Thus, each sixty-year cycle combines the 12 animals with five aspects that reflect the five elements (5 x 12 = 60 years).

Analyzing the Four Pillars requires an investigation of the elements symbolized by the two characters of each of the four pillars. These two characters are the heavenly stems and the earthly branches. The elements of earthly branches and heavenly stems have equal significance, and they influence the Feng Shui of any home. They can be enhanced for the person, and energizing the two elements creates good earth luck and excellent heavenly luck.

The simplest way to practice this method of Feng Shui is to find out which two elements are featured in your year pillar, after which you should proceed to energize the corresponding elements indicated in your home. It is that simple. The table overleaf offers the elements of the heavenly stem and earthly branch for those born in 1924, the year of the Rat, through to the year 1996, the year of the Boar. I have not gone further, since this method of Feng Shui is not especially useful for children or those deemed to be not adult – in Chinese tradition, only those who have married are said to be adults.

DISCOVERING YOUR EARTHLY BRANCH AND HEAVENLY STEM: 1924 TO 1960

DATE OF BIRTH	EARTHLY BRANCH (ELEMENT)	HEAVENLY STEM (ELEMENT)	SECTORS TO ACTIVATE
5 February 1924 – 23 January 1925	Rat (water)	wood	S, SE, E
24 January 1925 – 12 February 1926	Ox (earth)	wood	SW, NE, SE, E
13 February 1926 – 1 February 1927	Tiger (wood)	fire	SE, E, S
2 February 1927 – 22 January 1928	Rabbit (wood)	fire	SE, E, S
23 January 1928 – 9 February 1929	Dragon (earth)	earth	SW, NE
10 February 1929 – 29 January 1930	Snake (fire)	earth	S, SW, NE
30 January 1930 – 16 February 1931	Horse (fire)	metal	S, W, NW
17 February 1931 – 5 February 1932	Sheep (earth)	metal	SW, NE, W, NW
6 February 1932 – 25 January 1933	Monkey (metal)	water	W, NW, N
26 January 1933 – 13 February 1934	Rooster (metal)	water	W, NW, N
14 February 1934 – 3 February 1935	Dog (earth)	wood	SW, NE, SE, E
4 February 1935 – 23 January 1936	Boar (water)	wood	S, SE, E
24 January 1936 – 10 February 1937	Rat (water)	fire	N, S
11 February 1937 – 30 January 1938	Ox (earth)	fire	SW, NE, S
31 January 1938 – 18 February 1939	Tiger (wood)	earth	SE, E, SW, NE
19 February 1939 – 7 February 1940	Rabbit (wood)	earth	E, SE, SW, NE
8 February 1940 – 26 January 1941	Dragon (earth)	metal	SW, NE, W, NW
27 January 1941 – 14 February 1942	Snake (fire)	metal	S, W, NW
15 February 1942 – 4 February 1943	Horse (fire)	water	S, N
5 February 1943 – 24 January 1944	Sheep (earth)	water	SW, NE, N
25 January 1944 – 12 February 1945	Monkey (metal)	wood	NW, W, E, SE
13 February 1945 – 1 February 1946	Rooster (metal)	wood	W, NW, E, SE
2 February 1946 – 21 January 1947	Dog (earth)	fire	SW, NE, S
22 January 1947 – 9 February 1948	Boar (water)	fire	N, S
10 February 1948 – 28 January 1949	Rat (water)	earth	N, SW, NE
29 January 1949 – 16 February 1950	Ox (earth)	earth	SW, NE
17 February 1950 – 5 February 1951	Tiger (wood)	metal	SE, E, W, NW
6 February 1951 – 26 January 1952	Rabbit (wood)	metal	SE, E, W, NW
27 January 1952 – 13 February 1953	Dragon (earth)	water	SW, NE, N
14 February 1953 – 2 February 1954	Snake (fire)	water	S, N
3 February 1954 – 23 January 1955	Horse (fire)	wood	S, SE, E
24 January 1955 – 11 February 1956	Sheep (earth)	wood	SW, NE, SE, E
12 February 1956 – 30 January 1957	Monkey (metal)	fire	W, NW, S
31 January 1957 – 17 February 1958	Rooster (metal)	fire	W, NW, S
18 February 1958 – 7 February 1959	Dog (earth)	earth	SW, NE
8 February 1959 – 27 January 1960	Boar (water)	earth	SW, NE, N

DATE OF BIRTH	EARTHLY BRANCH (ELEMENT)	HEAVENLY STEM (ELEMENT)	SECTORS TO ACTIVATE
28 January 1960 – 14 February 1961	Rat (water)	metal	N, W, NW
15 February 1961 – 4 February 1962	Ox (earth)	metal	SW, NE, NW, W
5 February 1962 – 24 January 1963	Tiger (wood)	water	SE, E, N
25 January 1963 – 12 February 1964	Rabbit (wood)	water	SE, E, N
13 February 1964 – 1 February 1965	Dragon (earth)	wood	SW, NE, SE, E
2 February 1965 – 20 January 1966	Snake (fire)	wood	S, SE, E
21 January 1966 – 8 February 1967	Horse (fire)	fire	S
9 February 1967 – 29 January 1968	Sheep (earth)	fire	SW, NE, S
30 January 1968 – 16 February 1969	Monkey (metal)	earth	NW, W, SW, NE
17 February 1969 – 5 February 1970	Rooster (metal)	earth	NW, W, SW, NE
6 February 1970 – 26 January 1971	Dog (earth)	metal	SW, NE, NW, W
27 January 1971 – 14 February 1972	Boar (water)	metal	N, NW, W
15 February 1972 – 2 February 1973	Rat (water)	water	N
3 February 1973 – 22 January 1974	Ox (earth)	water	SW, NE, N
23 January 1974 – 10 February 1975	Tiger (wood)	wood	SE, E
11 February 1975 – 30 January 1976	Rabbit (wood)	wood	SE, E
31 January 1976 – 17 February 1977	Dragon (earth)	fire	SW, NE, S
18 February 1977 – 6 February 1978	Snake (fire)	fire	S
7 February 1978 – 27 January 1979	Horse (fire)	earth	S, SW, NE
28 January 1979 – 15 February 1980	Sheep (earth)	earth	SW, NE
16 February 1980 – 4 February 1981	Monkey (metal)	metal	W, NW
5 February 1981 – 24 January 1982	Rooster (metal)	metal	W, NW
25 January 1982 – 12 February 1983	Dog (earth)	water	SW, NE, N
13 February 1983 – 1 February 1984	Boar (water)	water	N
2 February 1984 – 19 February 1985	Rat (water)	wood	N, SE, E
20 February 1985 – 8 February 1986	Ox (earth)	wood	SW, NE, SE, E
9 February 1986 – 28 January 1987	Tiger (wood)	fire	SE, E, S
29 January 1987 – 16 February 1988	Rabbit (wood)	fire	SE, E, S
17 February 1988 – 5 February 1989	Dragon (earth)	earth	SW, NE
6 February 1989 – 26 January 1990	Snake (fire)	earth	S, SW, NE
27 January 1990 – 14 February 1991	Horse (fire)	metal	S, W, NW
15 February 1991 – 3 February 1992	Sheep (earth)	metal	SW, NE, NW, W
4 February 1992 – 22 January 1993	Monkey (metal)	water	W, NW, N
23 January 1993 – 9 February 1994	Rooster (metal)	water	W, NW, N
10 February 1994 – 30 January 1995	Dog (earth)	wood	SW, NE, SE, E
31 January 1995 – 18 February 1996	Boar (water)	wood	N, SE, E

EXAMINING THE HOUR PILLAR

In addition to analyzing the year pillar, it is useful to examine the hour pillar since this provides additional clues as to what would be beneficial for the person. The table opposite offers the corresponding earthly branch element for each of the 12 two-hour time slots. Please note that the hours are given a Yin or Yang dimension depending on whether it is night or daytime. Those born in the night-time hours will have more Yin in their time of birth, while those born in the daytime will have more Yang. This is neither good nor bad. It only offers clues for the overall reading. Thus if the other pillars show too much Yang then a balance of Yin energy during the time of birth will be auspicious and this should also be reflected in the arrangement and design of a room's decor.

EXAMINING THE MONTH PILLAR

If you wish, you may at this stage examine the month pillar, too. This does not require extensive computations. What you need to do is simply determine the season in which the person was born and then analyze the influence of the seasons on the person's basket of elements. By now you already have the person's year and hour details, giving you an idea of the lack of or excess of any element.

Against this analysis now factor in the impact of the season on the date of birth and you will get an idea of the element that will strengthen the Feng Shui of the person. You can either strengthen the element that is dominant in the year pillar or you can use the basket of elements approach and figure out what is "missing."

EXCESS YANG ENERGY SHOULD BE BALANCED BY YIN ENERGY IN THE ARRANGEMENT AND DESIGN OF A ROOM'S DECOR. HERE THE SOFT, CURVY SHAPES AND MUTED COLORS EMPHASIZE THE YIN ASPECTS OF THE ROOM.

THE YIN AND YANG OF DECOR

Creating a balanced home environment is vital to harmonious living and to promoting good Feng Shui. First principles of home furnishings and decorations include balancing the Yin and Yang aspects, or enhancing one aspect over the other, depending on whether you wish to achieve a relaxing Yin style room or a more vibrant, stimulating Yang style room. Features associated with Yin and Yang are as follows:

YIN

Dark; quiet; soft, curvy shapes; muted colors, such as blue, gray, or black; objects to promote relaxation, such as cushions; flowers and plants; crystals.

YANG

Activity; angular objects; light; sharp style; bright colors, such as red; stimulating decor and objects, such as horse sculptures, since the horse is deemed to be a Yang animal.

ELEMENTS IN THE HOUR PILLAR

TIME OF BIRTH	ELEMENT	EARTHLY BRANCH	YIN OR YANG	COLORS AND DESIGNS TO USE
11 pm to 1 am	Water	Rat hour	Yin	Blue, black, water motifs
1 am to 3 am	Earth	Ox hour	Yin	Pebbles, ceramics, urns
3 am to 5 am	Wood	Tiger hour	Yin	Green, plants, furniture
5 am to 7 am	Wood	Rabbit hour	Yin	Flowers, flower motifs
7 am to 9 am	Earth	Dragon hour	Yang	Crystals, stones
9 am to 11 am	Fire	Snake hour	Yang	Lights, lamps, sun
11 am to 1 pm	Fire	Horse hour	Yang	Red, maroons, yellow
1 pm to 3 pm	Earth	Sheep hour	Yang	Yellow, ochers
3 pm to 5 pm	Metal	Monkey hour	Yang	White, gold, silver
5 pm to 7 pm	Metal	Rooster hour	Yang	Metallic, stereo systems
7 pm to 9 pm	Earth	Dog hour	Yin	Clay pots, marble
9 pm to 11 pm	Water	Boar hour	Yin	Watermotifs, blue

ELEMENTS IN THE MONTH PILLAR

SEASON	METAL	WOOD	WATER	FIRE
Spring	is dying	thrives	is weakening	is born
Summer	is born	is weakening	is dying	thrives
Autumn	thrives	is dying	is born	is weakening
Winter	is weakening	is born	thrives	is dying

ASTROLOGICAL SECTIONS OF THE HOME

There is another method of using an individual's date of birth to investigate which astrological sections of the home should be energized and strengthened or at least must not be afflicted. When these sections or zones are hurt by the presence of a toilet, a stove, or a storeroom,

that person could suffer illness and a chronic lack of confidence. When the affliction is particularly severe, there could be accidents or illness that can sometimes prove fatal.

The way to determine your particular astrological section is to find out your earthly branch or Chinese animal – *see* the table on pages 108–9. Each of these animals rules an astrological section of the home, and the practice of Four Pillars is based on how you energize this compass section.

The table opposite gives the exact location of each astrological compass section in terms of degrees. Check your animal sign and then determine your section. Please note that each section occupies only a 15-degree segment of the compass.

WHICH ASTROLOGICAL SECTION OF YOUR HOME SHOULD BE ENERGIZED? USE YOUR DATE OF BIRTH AND THE TABLE OPPOSITE TO FIND OUT.

IN AN APARTMENT OR HOUSE, IT IS IMPORTANT TO BEWARE OF LOCATING A TOILET, STOVE, OR STOREROOM IN YOUR ASTROLOGICAL SECTION.

DISCOVERING YOUR ASTROLOGICAL LOCATION

ANIMAL	ASTROLOGICAL SECTION IN 15-DEGREE SEGMENTS	ASTROLOGICAL LOCATION ACCORDING TO THE COMPASS
Rat	352.5 to 7.5 degrees	north
Ox	22.5 to 37.5 degrees	north-northeast
Tiger	52.5 to 67.5 degrees	east-northeast
Rabbit	82.5 to 97.5 degrees	east
Dragon	112.5 to 127.5 degrees	east-southeast
Snake	142.5 to 157.5 degrees	south-southeast
Horse	172.5 to 187.5 degrees	south
Sheep	202.5 to 217.5 degrees	south-southwest
Monkey	232.5 to 247.5 degrees	west-southwest
Rooster	262.5 to 277.5 degrees	west
Dog	292.5 to 307.5 degrees	west-northwest
Boar	322.5 to 337.5 degrees	north-northwest

FIRST FIND OUT YOUR EARTHLY BRANCH OR ANIMAL OF THE CHINESE ZODIAC – *SEE* THE TABLE ON PAGE 111. THEN CONSULT THE CHART ABOVE TO DETERMINE WHICH SECTION OF YOUR HOME SHOULD BE ENERGIZED.

Applying the Formula

O n a compass, the segments emanate from the center of the circle. The circle is superimposed onto the layout plan of the home. In the Four Pillars method, locating the astrological sections in the home identifies auspicious parts of the home corresponding to each of the astrological animals. This method is different from the Eight Mansions Formula, which uses the Lo Shu grid to demarcate sectors of the home.

In Four Pillars Feng Shui, it is important to note the segments assigned to each of the animals. The rat is placed north, the horse is south, the rabbit is in the east, and the rooster is in the west. Their "places" on the compass also reflects the element they each represent.

1 *Locate the center of your home on your layout plan, which must be drawn to scale.*

2 *Use a good Western-style compass to find the magnetic north. Get a compass that has the bearings written out in degrees to enable you to obtain an accurate reading.*

3 *With the north located, you can draw the north-south axis through the center point of your home.*

4 *From there you can also draw the east-west axis, also running through the center point.*

5 *With these two axes giving you the directions it is easy to mark out each astrological section of the 12 animals in accordance with the table on page 113.*

NOTES
- Please endeavor to be accurate in your demarcation of the astrological segments.

- It is easier to work with a proper layout plan that is drawn to scale because it allows you to make accurate readings of the compass.
- If there are two or more levels to the house, you can use exactly the same kind of analysis for every level in the building.

The interpretation of good or afflicted Feng Shui is based on two things: your animal sign and whether the the toilet, bathroom, or stove is bringing bad luck to your astrological section of the home.

Look at the sectional layout (opposite), which shows a toilet in the tiger section, a bathroom in the dragon section, and a stove in the rooster section. If there are members of the household born in the tiger, dragon, or rooster years, then according to the Four Pillars method they will suffer from illness Feng Shui since their astrological zone is being afflicted.

This example illustrates Feng Shui afflictions that need to be dealt with. The best way to deal with toilets and stoves being in the wrong place is obviously to relocate them, but if you cannot, then using mirrors can ameliorate the situation. To overcome the harmful effect of toilets in an inauspicious section hang a large mirror on the outward-facing door of the toilet room so that it seems to disappear or paint the inside part of the door a bright red to counter the toilet's bad energy.

EACH ANIMAL OF THE CHINESE ZODIAC OCCUPIES A SPECIFIC SEGMENT OF THE COMPASS, STARTING WITH RAT IN THE NORTH.

ENHANCING THE CHI

Use the Four Pillars method to enhance the Chi in the astrological section of your home. Use the appropriate element to enhance each section. For example, if you are born in the year of the rat, then your section is the north of the home, which you should energize with water. Do this by having a water feature somewhere inside the segment that marks out the rat's astrological section. The water feature will enhance the Feng Shui of anyone living in the home who is a rat. Do not do this, however, if this part of the home is a bedroom, since it is not advisable to have water in the bedroom. Likewise, do not do this if the Flying Star chart advises against water.

This method of Feng Shui is practiced in the Far East and is especially popular in Hong Kong and Singapore. It is considered to be a personalized technique that places weight on the year of birth rather than on the actual time and date. Feng Shui masters often use this as a "quick-fix" method to investigate homes of clients who are loud in their complaints of things going wrong.

This technique is excellent for investigating cases where sudden or severe illness befalls an occupant who has recently moved into a new home or has changed room. The cause is usually a "dragon in the toilet," which means that a toilet occupies the astrological section of the dragon, or "a rat on the stove," which means the stove has been located in the astrological section of the rat. In both instances, anyone born in the year of the dragon or rat will suffer from negative Feng Shui. If they are also born during the hours of the dragon or rat, the negative impact will be magnified. The remedy for this is immediately to hang a five-rod wind chime in this sector. If there is no one born in the year of the rat living in this home, it is not necessary to hang the wind chime.

Use the table on page 113 to ensure that nothing harmful is located in the relevant astrological section of your home that belongs to you.

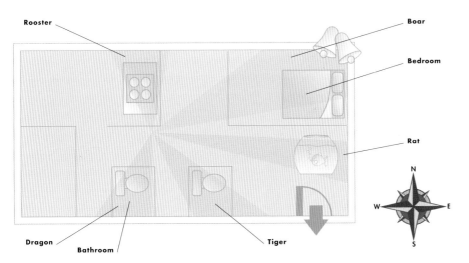

Rooster

Boar

Bedroom

Rat

Dragon

Bathroom

Tiger

THE TOILETS IN THE TIGER AND DRAGON SECTIONS AND STOVE IN THE ROOSTER SECTION MEAN HOUSEHOLD MEMBERS BORN IN TIGER, DRAGON, OR ROOSTER YEARS COULD SUFFER FROM ILLNESS FENG SHUI.
IF YOU ARE BORN IN A RAT YEAR, ENHANCE THE RAT'S ASTROLOGICAL SECTION OF THE HOUSE WITH A WATER FEATURE, E.G., AN AQUARIUM. IF YOU ARE BORN IN A BOAR YEAR, ENHANCE A BEDROOM IN THE BOAR'S ASTROLOGICAL SECTOR BY HANGING SMALL METALLIC BELLS TO ATTRACT GOOD FORTUNE.

8

THE WATER DRAGON FORMULA

The flow of wind and water manifest the physical effects of Feng Shui with both having the capability to bring good fortune. The direction water flows out of, around, and away from your home has a huge bearing on the flow of wealth Chi in the home. Ensure a good flow of Chi in and around your home and you will entice good fortune to enter; stifle it and losses will be the result. The direction the main door faces is central to this formula; once this has been established, all the correct and auspicious flows are revealed. The ultimate application of the Water Formula is to build an appropriate Water Dragon in the garden; you have to determine if this is a practical way for you to attract outstanding good fortune.

Feng Shui and Water

n Feng Shui analysis, the flow of water is said to mirror the flow of invisible Chi currents that move around the earth, bringing with it the potential for wealth and prosperity. The ancient texts describe in lyrical terms all the manifestations of good fortune that "good sentiment" water brings. These descriptions liken the good fortune to a dry tree blossoming once more, to branches and leaves being reborn, to the dragon quenching his thirst – all of which indicate misfortunes easily turning into good fortune.

Water is believed to exert the most significant influence on money luck. It can bring prosperity, but it can also be the cause of severe money loss. At its most simplistic level, water Feng Shui technology maintains that water flowing toward you or your main door brings you money, while water that is flowing away from your main door takes away all your money.

So water features, be they natural or artificial, should not be perceived to be flowing away. Waterfalls, pools, and fountains have no Feng Shui enhancing value unless the water has the appearance of coming toward the main door. Fountains and the like are, however, excellent for overcoming certain bad Flying Stars.

Meanwhile, rivers and canals that flow past your home bring better luck when they flow in front of the home than behind it. Only when the main door can see the flow of water will it manifest the potential of wealth luck.

THE FIVE ELEMENTS THEORY AND WATER

Water is one of the five elements that feature in the analysis and application of many Feng Shui formulas. The other four elements are fire, wood, metal, and earth. Understanding the significance of water and the way it relates to these four elements underscores the practice of prosperity Feng Shui. The "shui" of *Feng Shui* also means water.

In the five element theory, water is said to be produced by metal thus exhausting it. Water in turn produces wood and is exhausted by it. These two points are taken from the productive cycle of the five elements. In the

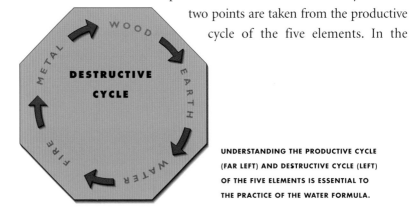

UNDERSTANDING THE PRODUCTIVE CYCLE (FAR LEFT) AND DESTRUCTIVE CYCLE (LEFT) OF THE FIVE ELEMENTS IS ESSENTIAL TO THE PRACTICE OF THE WATER FORMULA.

destructive cycle, water is destroyed by earth while it in turn destroys fire.

These element relationships become crucial in the application of any Feng Shui formula of the Compass School simply because every direction of the compass is representative of one of these five elements. Water is representative of the north. Irrespective of where in the world you are – be it in Australia, Europe, South America or Canada – the north is the place in your compass that represents water. Each of the four elements and their matching directions are shown on page 65. It is good Feng Shui to ensure element harmony at all times in the placement of your water features.

WATCHPOINT

A water dragon is a winding waterway that may end in a waterfall or a fountain or a pond ... anything winding (road, mountain range) represents a dragon.

RIVERS AND CANALS THAT FLOW PAST YOUR HOME BRING BETTER LUCK WHEN THEY FLOW IN FRONT OF THE HOME THAN BEHIND IT.

LANDSCAPE FENG SHUI AND WATER

There are two ways to look at Feng Shui and water. The Landscape School requires an assessment of the physical characteristics of water, for example, a river. It is necessary to consider its shape, its width, the quality of its water, the speed of its flow, the sharpness of its angles and turns, the color of the water, its freshness, and cleanliness to determine if it has the potential to bring good Feng Shui.

The best types of water are slow moving and clean. Rivers that meander gently past and in full view of the main door bring excellent Feng Shui. In Landscape Feng Shui this means that the river flows gently past the home in the lower land below, also described as "wearing a jade belt." Such a configuration is believed to bring prosperity to the family that will last through several generations.

COMPASS FENG SHUI AND WATER

Under Compass School Feng Shui, the location and direction of the flow of the water are determined according to the orientation of the main door and not the dates of birth of individual occupants. The Water Feng Shui Formula works with homes and their orientations. It is geared more toward the landscape than to the astrological aspects of Feng Shui. Thus, whether or not the flow of water should be from right to left or from left to right past the main door depends on the exact orientation of the main door of the home. This is indicated in the box below.

There are relationships between the different compass sectors in terms of the five elements. In addition, there are also intricate relationships between the respective trigrams that symbolize each sector and direction. For advanced practice, these need to be investigated, taking account of the Yin/Yang balance between the elements and the structures of the surrounding landscape.

Having to do all these things is what can make the practice of Feng Shui so very complex. I have discovered, however, that in amateur practice, going so deep into the practice offers only marginal benefits. Advanced Feng Shui is for the Feng Shui consultant, whose knowledge needs to be broad based and wide ranging to be able to advise on all manner of water orientations and flows.

For the amateur working on his or her own home, the important part of the exercise is to make sure the water flows are moving in the auspicious direction. This refers to the direction that water flows past the main door and out of the land. Taking this approach allows the Water Formula to be applied using a cookbook recipe approach that is both simple and effective.

Usually, when a home has good water Feng Shui everyone benefits. Water is magnanimous and generous. It is not a personalized practice meant only to benefit one person. Anyone staying in a home with good water flows will benefit from auspicious Feng Shui.

Inputs from both schools of Feng Shui should, as far as is practicable, be followed when applying the Water Formula. Thus, the orientations, directions, and locations of water should be figured out and the quality of the water observed. Always make sure that element harmony is maintained. Follow these basic guidelines if you wish to create auspicious Feng Shui.

1 *Take the direction of the main door correctly before you start. Remember that direction is always taken inside looking out.*

2 *Mark out the different compass sections of your surrounding land. You must be fully aware of your orientations if you want to use Compass Formula Feng Shui. Use a layout plan drawn to scale for this purpose.*

WATER FLOW AND THE MAIN DOOR

WATER SHOULD FLOW FROM RIGHT TO LEFT WHEN THE MAIN DOOR IS ORIENTED TO FACE:	WATER SHOULD FLOW FROM LEFT TO RIGHT WHEN THE MAIN DOOR IS ORIENTED TO FACE:
southwest	south
northwest	north
southeast	east
northeast	west

3 *When water flow has to turn to accommodate the lay of the land, try as much as possible to make the angle of flow match the element of its location. For example, in the sectors east and southeast, which is the wood sector, use an angle of flow that reflects either the wood angle or the water angle (because water produces wood and is thus harmonious).*

THE WATER FORMULA IN FENG SHUI

The ancient texts on water and in particular the *Water Dragon Classic* differentiates between big water and small water.

Big water refers to natural bodies of water in the environment; rivers, lakes, ponds, mining pools, and even the seas and oceans constitute big water. If you are fortunate enough to be living in the vicinity of a natural body of water, the use of the Water Formula enables you to "tap" it, so that it brings you great prosperity. The secret to doing this lies in the way you orientate your home, especially the way you position and orientate the main front door.

Small water, on the other hand, refers to the artificial water flows constructed by people. These are water courses, both private and public, and also wells and fish ponds. These take the place of big water and are equally potent and effective if there is a constant flow and supply of water. It is by building water courses around the home that the Water Formula can be harnessed to bring prosperity and wealth luck. But do remember that a water course only works when it is filled with moving water. If your water course dries up or the water stays stagnant, it represents a dead dragon, which brings bad luck.

Irrespective of whether the water is small or big, there are three major determinants that affect the prosperity potential of the flow of water around the home:
- the way it flows past the main door
- the way it flows around the home
- the way it flows out of your land or property.

The Water Formula offers specific instructions on all three of these factors. How the water should flow depends on the direction of the main door and in some cases also on the contours of the land on which the home stands. To simplify the application of this formula I have arranged it in accordance with 12 specific categories of door directions. The three good fortune exit directions for each category are then summarized. Whenever possible, you should make certain that the direction of your water course out of the home is only in one of the auspicious directions. All other directions result in varying degrees of misfortune, and among them are two that result in severe disaster befalling the family.

THE 12 CATEGORIES OF DOOR DIRECTIONS ARE BASED ON THE 24 DOOR DIRECTIONS DERIVED BY HAVING THREE SUBDIRECTIONS FOR EVERY MAIN DIRECTION. OF THE 24 SUBDIRECTIONS, EVERY TWO SUBDIRECTION SECTORS MERGE TO BECOME A SINGLE DOOR CATEGORY.

CASE STUDY 1

If your door faces 180 degrees from north then it is facing the Wu direction and your door belongs to category 1. This category door direction requires the water to flow past the front door from left to right. This means that when you are standing inside the door looking out, the water should be flowing from left to right.

The best exit flow of water for category 1 homes is toward the sin or shih direction, meaning it should flow out at an angle of between 277.5 and 307.5 degrees (see Summary opposite). The best way to simulate this auspicious flow of water is to build a small water course in that direction. When designing drains to tap the correct exit directions, try to be accurate, since exiting in the sector next to an auspicious sector is often the cause of great misfortunes. So be very, very accurate.

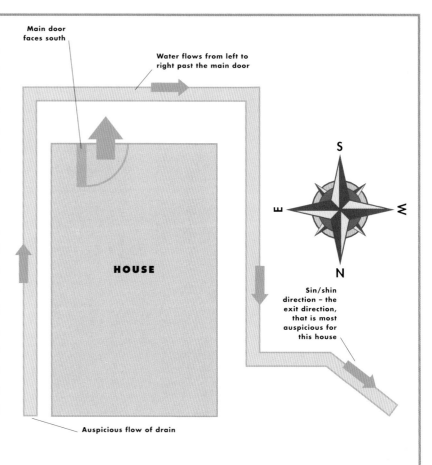

Main door faces south

Water flows from left to right past the main door

HOUSE

Sin/shin direction – the exit direction, that is most auspicious for this house

Auspicious flow of drain

CASE STUDY 2

If your door is facing the sin direction, i.e., between 277.5 and 292.5 degrees, your home is regarded as a category 5 home. This means that standing inside looking out of your main front door you will be facing west-northwest. The water in front of your home should then flow from right to left. The next thing to determine is the ideal exit direction of water from your home to make the flow auspicious. Based on the formula, you will see that the best exit direction is southwest, i.e., in the kun/sen direction, which lies in the angle between 217.5 to 247.5 degrees. Once again, the best way to achieve this flow of water is to use the drainage system around the home. But make sure your drains always have a flow of water. Stagnant and dry drains indicate a "dead dragon."

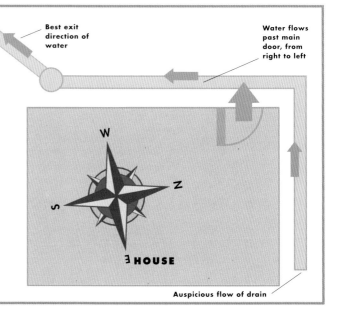

Best exit direction of water

Water flows past main door, from right to left

HOUSE

Auspicious flow of drain

A SUMMARY OF THE WATER FORMULA

TWELVE DOOR CATEGORIES	DIRECTION THE DOOR FACES	SUBDIRECTION NAMES AND DEGREES ON COMPASS	FLOW OF WATER PASS MAIN DOOR	BEST EXIT DIRECTIONS 1ST, 2ND, AND 3RD
1	South	Ping: 157.5 to 172.5 degrees Wu: 172.5 to 187.5 degrees	Left to right	1st: via sin or shih 2nd: via ting or wei 3rd: via chia
2	South-southwest	Ting: 187.5 to 202.5 degrees Wei: 202.5 to 217.5 degrees	Right to left	1st: via shun or tze 2nd: via kun 3rd: not available*
3	Southwest	Kun : 217.5 to 232.5 degrees Sen: 232.5 to 247.5 degrees	Right to left	1st: via yi or shen 2nd: via ting or wei 3rd: via ken or yu
4	West	Ken: 247.5 to 262.5 degrees Yu: 262.5 to 277.5 degrees	Left to right	1st: via kway or choh 2nd: via sin or shih 3rd: via ping
5	West-northwest	Sin: 277.5 to 292.5 degrees Shih: 292.5 to 307.5 degrees	Right to left	1st: via kun or sen 2nd: via chien or hai 3rd: not available*
6	Northwest	Chian: 307.5 to 322.5 degrees Hai: 322.5 to 352.5 degrees	Right to left	1st: via ting or wei 2nd: via sin or shih 3rd: via zen or cher
7	North	Zen: 352.5 to 367.5 degrees Cher: 367.5 to 7.5 degrees	Left to right	1st: via yi or shen 2nd: via kway or choh 3rd: via ken
8	North-northeast	Kway: 7.5 to 22.5 degrees Choh: 22.5 to 37.5 degees	Right to left	1st: via chian or hai 2nd: via gen or yin 3rd: not available*
9	Northeast	Gen: 37.5 to 52.5 degrees Yin: 52.5 to 67.5 degrees	Right to left	1st: via sin or shih 2nd: via kway or choh 3rd: via chia or mau
10	East	Chia: 67.5 to 82.5 degrees Mau: 82.5 to 97.5 degrees	Left to right	1st: via ting or wei 2nd: via yi or shen 3rd: via zen
11	East-southeast	Yi: 97.5 to 112.5 degrees Shen: 112.5 to 127.5 degrees	Right to left	1st: via gen or yin 2nd: via shun or tze 3rd: not available*
12	Southeast	Shun: 127.5 to 142.5 degrees Tze : 142.5 to 157.5 degrees	Right to left	1st: via kway or choh 2nd: via yi or shen 3rd: via ping or wu

*No auspicious third option is available – see "Selecting Exit Directions," page 124

Applying the Formula

When you have ascertained exactly which subdirection your door faces and used the table on the previous page to discover the best exit directions and water flows past your main door, you can begin applying the formula. Usually there are three good exit directions listed, but you need not feel obliged to go with the first. If this is not possible, look at the second or even the third direction. They bring good fortune as well. The text below explains the differences between the directions and what you can aspire to.

SELECTING EXIT DIRECTIONS

1 The first exit direction of each door category offers three combinations of luck. Precious jewels are said to flow unceasingly to the residents, and the master or patriarch of the household will wear a jade belt around his waist – symbolic of great wealth and power. He will enjoy an elevated status in society and become a powerful and respected member of the establishment. Prosperity luck is exceptional, and there will be great abundance of money. In addition, such a home will have many descendants, who will be loyal and bring honor to the family name. All the sons and daughters will be intelligent, and this flow of water will be equally beneficial for both the men and women of the household. In short, the first exit direction indicates every type of luck flowing into the home.

2 If it is not possible to tap this first direction, going for the second exit direction also brings good fortune. A home that enjoys this exit flow will definitely become a rich home and the men in the family will succeed in getting a high position with the government. Residents of such an abode will benefit from good health. Money luck brings enhanced incomes, and even during bad times your good Feng Shui will protect you from suffering excessive losses.

3 Selecting which exit direction to use depends entirely on your particular situation and it is sometimes not possible to tap the first or second best directions. However, I have been assured by the Feng Shui master who gave me this Water Formula that even the third best direction usually brings extremely auspicious luck.

4 However, there are four door categories when the third exit direction brings grave misfortunes:

- In door categories 2, 5, and 8, the third water exit direction brings poverty and a breakdown of family fortunes.
- In door category 11, the third exit direction brings a mixture of good and bad luck, which ultimately leads to a bad ending for the residents in the home.

In these four door categories, therefore, the option of good exit flow is limited to a choice between one and two. In the reference table on page 123, I have indicated the third water exit direction as not available for the door categories that do not have an auspicious third option of water flow.

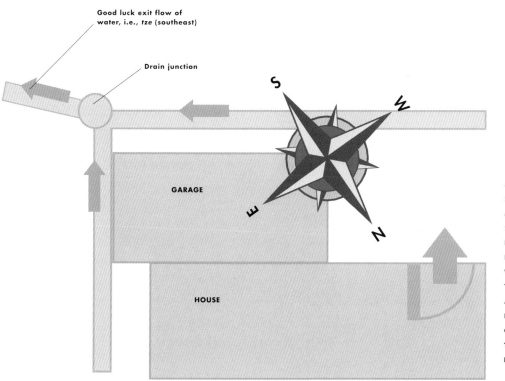

Good luck exit flow of
water, i.e., *tze* (southeast)

Drain junction

S

W

E

N

GARAGE

HOUSE

MAIN DOOR FACES SOUTH-
SOUTHWEST, I.E., TING,
MAKING THIS A CATEGORY
2 HOUSE. IN THIS
EXAMPLE, THE WATER IN
FRONT OF THE MAIN DOOR
WAS FLOWING FROM LEFT
TO RIGHT AND THIS WAS
ASCERTAINED TO BE
INAUSPICIOUS, SO A NEW
COURSE HAD TO BE BUILT
TO LET THE WATER FLOW
FROM RIGHT TO LEFT.

ACCOMMODATING THE WATER FORMULA

Overcoming obstacles in the application of the formula often requires creativity and a genuine determination to create exactly the right kind of water flow. This is because you might have to endure a certain amount of inconvenience to accommodate the guidelines. Sometimes drains have to be completely rebuilt. Or when the contours of the home are sloping in the wrong direction, a certain amount of digging and recontouring might become necessary if the drains are to flow in the correct direction around the home.

In addition, in order to maximize the benefits of the exit flow, as much of the water as possible from the home and around the home should exit via the auspicious direction.

Please always remember that the angle of the outward water flow must be absolutely correctly oriented. This is the most important part of the formula and if you are using a contractor, you should make certain that someone reliable is supervising the job. Do not take it for granted that the job will be done correctly. I know of cases where the angle of flow comes out wrong even after the Feng Shui master went personally to check the angle with his compass a few times.

Consider covering the well to prevent anyone from falling into it. However, if your drains have been built for Feng Shui reasons, they should be visible from the sky, otherwise they lose their Feng Shui significance and the exercise is wasted. Use an iron grating to cover deep drains and wells. These allow the drains and therefore the flow of water to be visible.

Water Dragons in the Garden

Probably the most exciting application of the Water Formula is the construction of artificial Water Dragons to attract outstanding good fortune, which is said to last for seven generations and beyond. Water Dragons cannot be auspiciously built for all of the door categories. This section describes the potential for building Water Dragons in seven categories of door directions – from door category 5 to door category 12.

Water dragons in the garden are not necessarily better than using the first exit direction. Although a Water Dragon seems to promise so much, I urge some caution. While the impact of getting it right is wonderful prosperity, the result of getting it wrong can be disastrous – and it is quite easy to get it wrong. In my own home I use the first exit direction of the formula and I am perfectly happy with the results. The terrain of my land is unsuitable for a Water Dragon. On the other hand, a friend built a Water Dragon shortly after I presented her with my Water Feng Shui book three years ago. Today, her husband has reached multimillionaire status several

WATER DRAGONS IN THE GARDEN ARE NOT NECESSARILY BETTER THAN USING THE FIRST EXIT DIRECTION.

times over and they were also not affected by the severe economic problems that hit Asia in mid-1997.

In addition, the Water Formula texts describe at great length what kind of family or patriarch has the "heaviness" to maintain a Water Dragon. In other words, unless you have the heaven luck to benefit from a Water Dragon, it might be better not to have one built. On the other hand, if you do have the heaven luck to benefit from a Water Dragon, then having one built in the garden of your home brings enormous benefits for many generations.

Only those with sufficient land can consider building a Water Dragon. This is therefore not an option for everyone. Nor can everyone even afford to have one built. For corporate and national developments, however, building a Water Dragon can bring enormous success to the project. It is therefore advisable to consider this part of the Water Formula as being suitable for large and ambitious projects that bring great benefits to many people.

Some of the guidelines for building a Water Dragon are relatively simple while others are very difficult. It all depends on the orientation of the main entrance door.

WATER DRAGON FOR A CATEGORY 5 BUILDING

A category 5 building has the main door directly facing the sin/shih direction (west-northwest and between 277.5 and 307.5 degrees). To create a most auspicious Water Dragon, which brings enormous prosperity, use the following directions. It is important to build the flow of water correctly.

1 Let the water come from the direction of sin, i.e., west-northwest. (277.9 to 292.5 degrees) (see below).

2 Let the water flow from left to right past the main door (see below).

3 Then let the water circle around at least part of the building and flow toward the direction of east.

4 Finally, let the water exit in a chia direction, that is, flowing directly east between 67.5 and 82.5 degrees.

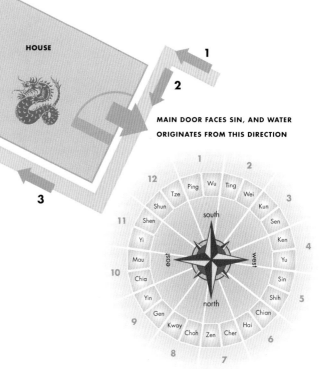

HOUSE

MAIN DOOR FACES SIN, AND WATER ORIGINATES FROM THIS DIRECTION

WATER DRAGON FOR A CATEGORY 6 BUILDING

A category 6 building has the main door facing any direction between 307.5 and 352.5 degrees, or directly in the northwest direction (the chian or hai direction). The potential for building a Water Dragon exists provided the contours of the land allow it. Here the land to the right of the garden, if standing inside the building and looking out, must be slightly elevated. If you can succeed in building this Water Dragon and follow the directions diligently, there will be great good fortune and everything undertaken by members of the household or building will be successful. Money pours into the household and every kind of good fortune is evident. Here are the directions:

1 *Water must flow from a height toward the main door (see below).*

2 *Then it must flow past the main door moving from right to left.*

3 *After that the water must flow out of the garden or land in a hai direction. This means the flow must be in the northwest direction at an angle between 322.5 and 352.5 degrees. The water will seem to be flowing out of the garden directly in front of the main door.*

4 *Let the water flow in this direction flow for about 100 ft (30 m) and then let it loop back in any direction. As long as the water appears to flow back toward the home a Water Dragon has been created.*

5 *After flowing back, allow the water to flow out of the land unseen. This means the water must go underground after it loops back. The symbolic meaning is that the water (representing wealth) simply accumulates in the home and never flows out.*

HOUSE

5

4 MAIN DOOR FACES CHIAN/HAI DIRECTION

3

2

1

ELEVATED LAND

south

east   west

north

1 — Wu, Ting
Ping, Wei
12 — Tze
Shun, Kun
11 — Shen, Sen
Yi, Ken
Mau, Yu
10 — Chia, Sin
Yin, Shih
Gen, Chian
9 — Kway, Hai
Choh, Zen, Cher
8

2
3
4
5
6
7

WATER DRAGON FOR A CATEGORY 7 BUILDING

In a category 7 home, the main door faces the zen or cher direction, which is basically the north direction. The exact bearing is between 352.5 and 7.5 degrees on the compass. The potential for building a Water Dragon for such a home exists if there is at least 100 ft (30 m) of space in the northeast sector of the yard since one of the requirements for the water flow is for it to move at least 100 ft (30 m) in the northeast direction.

If yours is a category 7 home and you can succeed in building this Water Dragon around your home, you and your family will enjoy great prosperity and abundance. Everything good will flow into the home. There will be good business luck, and many opportunities for making money will flow to the residents. If the terrain is also favorable, the family patriarch will even achieve ministerial status. The children of the family will prosper, too, and bring great honor to the family name. Here are the directions for creating a category 7 Water Dragon.

1 *Let water flow past the main door from right to left.*

2 *Then let the water seem to exit in a gen direction. The angle of the outflow is between 37.5 and 52.5 degrees. Let the water flow like this for 100 ft (30 m).*

3 *Then let the water turn around toward the left, thereby forming a loop or curve.*

4 *Let the water flow on but camouflage it after this – don't show the water leaving the garden.*

IN A CATEGORY 7 HOME YOU CAN ONLY BUILD A WATER DRAGON IF THERE IS AT LEAST 100 FT (30 M) OF SPACE IN THE NORTHEAST SECTOR SINCE THIS IS NEEDED FOR THE WATER FLOW.

WATER DRAGONS FOR A CATEGORY 8 BUILDING

If yours is a category 8 home, you have two Water Dragon options. A category 8 home has its main door facing either kway or choh, which is north-northeast in terms of compass direction. The exact compass reading is that the door direction lies between 7.5 and 37.5 degrees. Before you go overboard and start construction immediately, first investigate the terrain of your land. The water manual states that land which is excessively hilly is unsuitable for Water Dragons. Also, certain angles of flow are to be strenuously avoided, in which case it could be advisable to stick to the first and second exit directions given in the table on page 123 and not attempt to build a Water Dragon. The choice is left to you. Investigate your land and the space you have before you decide. If you choose to build a Water Dragon, make certain that the compass reading of your exit direction is accurate.

WATCHPOINT

Land that is excessively hilly is usually unsuitable for building Water Dragons.

WATER DRAGON NUMBER ONE

If successfully constructed, this Water Dragon brings BIG money luck. Children are filial and will prosper. Businesses will expand and there is elevation of rank for the head of the household. Extremely good fortune will be the result. Here are the directions:

1 *Let the water flow past the main door from left to right.*

2 *Then let it flow out in a kway direction, i.e., at an angle bearing between 7.5 and 22.5 degrees from the north, and very near the main door. It must not touch the choh direction (between 22.5 and 37.5 degrees) so the compass direction taken must be accurate and in the actual construction you must be very careful.*

3 *Then let the water continue to flow for 100 ft (30 m) in the kway direction before letting it turn toward the right.*

Main door faces kway/choh direction

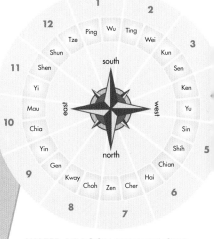

WATER DRAGON NUMBER ONE FOR A CATEGORY 8 BUILDING

WATER DRAGON NUMBER TWO

If successfully constructed, this Water Dragon brings five generations of good fortune. Money flows in easily and everything meets with success. However, it cannot work on hilly or mountainous land. The surface area of the land must be completely flat otherwise the dragon simply cannot come alive and there cannot be good fortune. The directions are as follows:

1 *Let the water flow past the main door from left to right. The water is coming from the kway direction.*

2 *Then let it turn right and go around the home.*

3 *Finally, let the water flow out via the ping direction in the south (at the back of the home). This means the water must flow out at an angle of between 157.5 and 172.5 degrees. But in so doing it must not touch wu direction, which is just next to ping (between 172.5 and 178.5 degrees).*

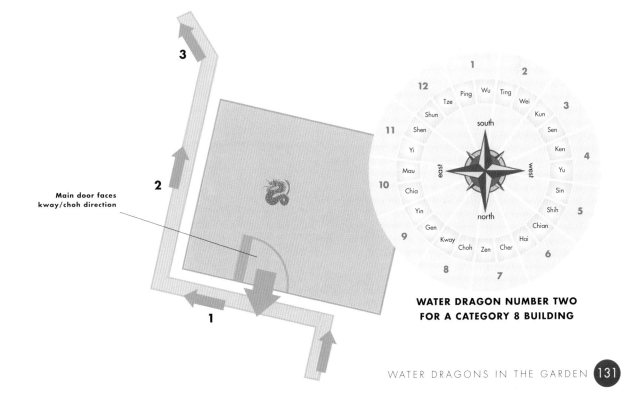

Main door faces
kway/choh direction

**WATER DRAGON NUMBER TWO
FOR A CATEGORY 8 BUILDING**

WATER DRAGON FOR A CATEGORY 9 BUILDING

If your main door faces the gen or yin direction (the northeast), an extremely auspicious Water Dragon can be constructed that will bring abundance and great prosperity. There will be good business luck and many opportunities for making money. If the terrain is favorable, the family will also enjoy great respectability with the patriarch achieving ministerial status. Children of the household will prosper and bring honor to the family name. All the residents of the home will benefit. The directions for the Water Dragon are as follows:

1 *Let the water flow past the main door from right to left.*

2 *Then let the water exit via the gen direction in the northeast and near the main door (between 37.5 and 52.5 degrees). When flowing out, the angle must not touch the yin direction (between 52.5 and 67.5 degrees). Let the water flow in this direction for 100 ft (30 m).*

3 *Finally, let the water loop around and turn to the left in a curve.*

SUCCESSFULLY BUILD A WATER DRAGON FOR A CATEGORY 9 HOME AND THE CHILDREN OF THE HOUSEHOLD WILL PROSPER.

WATER DRAGON FOR A CATEGORY 10 BUILDING

When your main door faces east, and more specifically when it faces between 67.5 and 97.5 degrees, which is called the chia and mau directions, you can transform the drains around your home into a powerful Water Dragon. When properly executed, this configuration of water flow brings big money into the household. There will be great wealth attracted to the home, which will benefit all the residents. Such a Water Dragon should be built on flat land and there should not be any stone or structure that resembles a hostile animal situated in the vicinity of the water course. Otherwise the Feng Shui will be affected negatively.

1 *Let the water flow from right to left past the main door.*

2 *Then let it flow out in a chia direction toward the east, between 67.5 and 82.5 degrees, just in front of the main door. When you build this water course, make very sure that the water does not flow out in a mau direction (between 82.5 and 97.5 degrees). It must not even touch the mau direction.*

3 *Let the water flow for about 100 ft (30 m), then let it turn around toward the left. It is unnecessary to worry about the angle.*

WATER DRAGONS FOR A CATEGORY 11 BUILDING

When your main door faces east-southeast, and more specifically when it faces between 97.5 and 127.5 degrees, which is called the yi and shen directions, there is potential to create two Water Dragon configurations of water flow, either of which spells excellent Feng Shui.

WATER DRAGON NUMBER ONE

This configuration of water flow brings great prosperity

luck. There is great wealth for members of the house-hold and the patriarch will attain high office in the land.

1 *Let the water flow from left to right past the main door.*

2 *Then let it flow outward in a yi direction at an angle between 97.5 to 112.5 degrees just in front of the main door.*

3 *Let the water flow on for about 100 ft (30 m), then let it turn toward the right. It is unnecessary to worry about the angle.*

WATER DRAGON NUMBER TWO

The requirement for this dragon is that the land must be flat, and then there will be fantastic luck if everything is done correctly. Prosperity and wealth are assured.

1 *Let the water originate from the yi direction at an angle of between 97.5 and 112.5 degrees.*

2 *Then let it turn right and flow toward the back of the home until it reaches the west sector.*

3 *Then let it flow out of the home compound via the ken direction between 247.5 and 262.5 degrees. In so doing, make sure you are perfectly accurate and that the angle of flow does not even touch the yu direction next to it (between 262.5 and 277.5 degrees).*

WATER DRAGON FOR A CATEGORY 12 BUILDING

When your main door faces southeast, and more specifically when it faces between 127.5 to 157.5 degrees, which is called the shun and tze directions, you can design a water configuration that taps into the Water

Dragon's prosperity luck. If this can be done correctly, great prosperity luck will be created for the household. Everything will seem to happen with ease. Money will flow in and the good fortune will last for a very long time, with the family attaining nobility status. This is considered a most auspicious configuration of water flow, which can be equally applied on flat or on undulating land. The drains around your home can be transformed into a powerful Water Dragon by following the directions given here:

1 *Let the water flow from right to left past the main door.*

2 *Then let it flow out in a shun direction at an angle between 127.5 to 142.5 degrees just in front of the main door. When you build this water course make sure that the water does not flow out in a tze direction just next to it.*

3 *Moving at this angle let the water flow for about 100 ft (30 m), then let the water turn around toward the left and let it slowly trickle into a smaller water flow.*

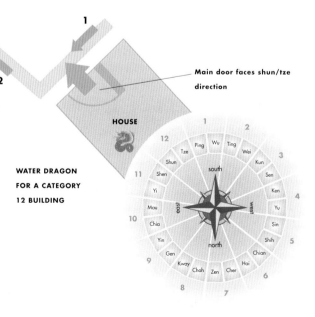

Main door faces shun/tze direction

HOUSE

WATER DRAGON FOR A CATEGORY 12 BUILDING

Afterword

Attempting to convey something of the powerful magic of Compass Formula Feng Shui in a condensed book that tries to make it easy to follow, understand, and practice can at best be only partially successful. There are so many perspectives and there is also such a great deal of mystical knowledge involved. I have decided that it is not necessary to try to comprehend *how* Formula Feng Shui works; instead, I think it is sufficient to follow the methods given in the old texts and to practice them as accurately as possible.

Some of the formulas are so complicated you may not find it possible to use them immediately. If this is the case, read through the relevant chapter again and try to practice the method given, step by step. If you find references to the five elements or to Yin and Yang cosmology too complex I recommend you get one of my introductory books on the subject (*see* Further Reading). With a good understanding of the fundamentals of Feng Shui your chances of success with the formulas will be vastly increased. In the interests of brevity, I have not described the more elementary aspects of Feng Shui practice in any detail in this book.

The good news, however, is that it is possible to leap from the theoretical underpinnings to the practice without sacrificing any of Feng Shui's effectiveness. This book condenses the formulas, making them user-friendly, yet effective for improving our lives. These formulas are effective and workable in creating the kind of luck that brings more wealth and greater ease of living. I have used them with varying degrees of success. You should never forget to factor in the fact that Feng Shui works in tandem with two other types of luck – the luck of heaven, which determines whether we can become seriously wealthy or merely rich, and humankind luck, which depends on our own efforts.

Of all the formulas in the book, the three formulas with greatest promise are the Eight Mansions Formula, the Flying Star Formula, and the Water Dragon Formula. You can follow the directions given with the confidence that they have been tried and tested by some of the best Feng Shui masters of this century.

Each one of the formulas can be practiced on its own, and this alone would bring stunningly good Feng Shui if you follow the directions correctly and your heaven luck is conducive to your enjoying great good fortune. Good Feng Shui speeds up the coming of good fortune and overcomes obstacles that block opportunities from ripening into good fortune.

They can also be used together. They need not, and should not, be seen as being contradictory. I know there may be instances when in following one formula, you clash with the recommendations of another. The initial reaction is confusion, anger, and frustration. In truth, though, apparently contradictory recommendations often hide deeper meanings. I have generally discovered, after discussion with my Feng Shui teachers, there is always an explanation for the apparent contradiction.

When you first start to work with Formula Feng Shui and find yourself in such a situation, choose the option that presents the fewest problems in execution. Also, between energizing for good luck or protecting yourself from bad luck, choose protection over the active enhancing agent that brings good luck, because no amount of Feng Shui energizing can work if your home, door, or sleeping direction is being afflicted with something harmful in the environment around you.

Putting the Formulas Together

Always start by taking a good look at the main door before studying each of the formulas to see how the direction and location of the main door affects all the Feng Shui considerations around the home. The best way is to check which directions and locations bring you and your family good luck. If you are the breadwinner, use your own direction to determine the ideal orientation of your main door, and, where possible, let the door face the direction that best suits you. This means bringing you good luck without it simultaneously causing you to incur something negative based on another school of Feng Shui. It is this juggling of methods that makes Feng Shui a complex practice for the amateur, but it also makes it fun. Practice is neither as complex nor as difficult as at first seems.

I find the best starting point is to arm myself with my personalized good and bad directions based on the East and West Group people theory of the Eight Mansions school. When you decide on door directions note two specific issues that may initially confuse you.

• The directions given in all the formulas is the same direction irrespective of where you live. They work equally well in Australia or Canada, in Europe or South Africa, and in North or South America. Thus be it in the Northern or Southern Hemisphere, the north referred to in Feng Shui is the magnetic north of the compass. There is no necessity to flip the directions around in your applications. Please do not do so, since by flipping the directions, everything in the formula has automatically gone wrong. If you want to flip the directions then I strongly suggest you do not use my formulas and instead use the formulas of those practitioners who advocate changing the direction in the Southern Hemisphere.

• All directions referred to are taken from just inside the door looking out. All references to left and right are also similarly taken from just inside the home looking outward. This is the base orientation in Feng Shui recommendations.

Once you have had your Eight Mansions directions and locations factored into your home, the next step is to calculate the Flying Star natal chart of your home. Use the reference tables to move out of afflicted rooms and enhance the use of lucky areas and try to involve the impact of the Flying Star Formula. The Lo Shu grid that identifies the problem areas of your home should never be forgotten.

You can use the five element theory of the Nine Aspirations Formula to energize the different corners of your home to activate different areas of luck. Feng Shui recognizes and differentiates between the many different aspirations of humankind and thus prescribes different methods for energizing different kinds of luck.

Probably the most important kind of luck that finds universal favor with one and all is that of prosperity luck. This refers to the enhancement of incomes and the creation of wealth. For this there is nothing to beat the Water Formula, which offers the secret techniques of building the Water Dragon in your own backyard. So, try to have an excellent main door – one that brings you loads of sheng chi luck – and then build a water flow that complements your good fortune main door. Combining the formulas in this way is extremely effective for enhancing the Feng Shui of your home.

Meet Lillian Too

Lillian Too was the first woman in Asia to become the Chief Executive Officer of a bank when, in 1982, she accepted the appointment of Managing Director of the Grindlays Dao Heng Bank in Hong Kong. Later, as Deputy Executive Chairman of Dickson Concepts, she worked closely with Dickson Poon, before acquiring and becoming Executive Chairman of her own chain of department stores, the Dragon Seed group of stores in Hong Kong.

In Malaysia, where she comes from, Lillian Too is described by *Malaysian Business*, the country's leading business magazine, as "something of a legend in corporate circles being the first woman there to become the Managing Director of a publicly listed company."

Lillian is an MBA graduate from the Harvard Business School, in Boston. She has been described as being "in a league of her own" by the country's leading *Success* magazine. The internationally acclaimed *Vogue* magazine describes her "as someone people listen to."

As a business woman, Lillian Too made enough money never to have to work again. In the early 1990s, she retired from working life to become a full-time mother. That was when she started a new career in writing. To date she has penned 18 international bestsellers, most of which are on her favorite subject of Feng Shui, which she says was responsible for giving her masses of luck in her corporate career and during her days as a business woman in Hong Kong. Lillian Too is married and has one daughter.

In 1997, the phenomenal worldwide success of her book *The Complete Illustrated Guide to Feng Shui*, published by Element Books of UK, USA, and Australia, made waves in the nonfiction book trade. The book is an international bestseller and has become the classic Feng Shui text. This has been followed by the bestselling *Feng Shui Kit* and *Feng Shui Fundamentals*. In November 1999, Element published her *Illustrated Encyclopedia of Feng Shui* and *Space Clearing Kit*. Both have elicited eager enthusiasm from her hundreds of thousands of fans worldwide. Lillian Too's Feng Shui books have now been translated into 18 languages and nearly two million copies of her books have been sold worldwide. This book is part of a new series called *Practical Feng Shui*.

LILLIAN TOO, DUBBED "THE PUBLIC FACE OF FENG SHUI WORLDWIDE," HAS WRITTEN 30 BOOKS ON FENG SHUI, 18 OF WHICH HAVE BECOME INTERNATIONAL BESTSELLERS.

A Sampling of What Others Say

Lillian Too's Feng Shui website has been big news. Feng Shui is the Chinese art of geomancy – a cross between psychic energy and interior design – and Lillian Too can make a Swiss ski chalet seem as spiritual as Stonehenge … in Asia she is a celebrity and her online consultations are burning up lots of Asian band-width.

WIRED, USA

Highly readable and with interesting anecdotes, Lillian Too's Feng Shui should interest everyone who seeks to understand the forces of Nature … it is an invaluable addition to the growing literature on Eastern thinking and Lillian Too is to be congratulated for her timely contribution.

DR. TARCISIUS CHIN, CEO

… Too is a person who practices what she preaches.

NEW STRAITS TIMES

… to the readers of her best selling books throughout Malaysia, Lillian Too has only just begun.

BUSINESS TIMES

Too's credentials are impeccable.

SARAWAK SUNDAY TRIBUNE

… she is not the sort of proponent of this ancient Chinese art who peddles her knowledge to companies … what she does, and has done with considerable success, is write books about Feng Shui.

SMART INVESTOR

Too distills the essence of the practice and explains in simple terms how Feng Shui can improve anyone's life.

VOGUE MAGAZINE

Personal Acknowledgment

My dear readers,

Three of the most important formulas contained in this book came to me directly from Master Yap Cheng Hai. When I tentatively suggested to him that we could pass on the secrets of the ancient Feng Shui formulas to the universality of humankind through my books, I only half expected Master Yap to say yes. My experience with Feng Shui masters in Hong Kong and Taiwan had taught me to expect a certain amount of reticence and reluctance when it comes to revealing comprehensive explanations of complicated formulas, techniques, and methods.

Master Yap's ready and generous acquiescence has made this and other books possible. I am deeply grateful to his generosity of spirit, not only because he magnanimously and universally shared his knowledge, but also because he went to great pains to translate and then patiently to explain the very complex and sometimes apparently conflicting insights given in the ancient texts.

In every single case of doubt or ambiguity, however, the solution always presented itself after much discussion and debate, and when this happened the particular guideline or rule in question became blazingly clear. Those were moments of sheer delight and undiluted pleasure, as we penetrated the veil of the language and symbolism locked within the ancient words.

If it were not for Master Yap's generosity, the key pieces of these formulas would never have become available. As those of you already familiar with the formulas have discovered, it was the seemingly small bits and pieces of information that provided such valuable keys to understanding whatever portions of the formulas had already been revealed to the world.

Many of those formulas released earlier had been incomplete. We should thus say silent words of thanks to Master Yap for his generosity in sharing his great knowledge with the world.

I also want to thank Element Books, my fabulous Publisher. In working with me, they have made Feng Shui so accessible and such a great joy to read about. The design, format, and selection of pictures have stayed true to the essence of Feng Shui and for this I am forever grateful. Element has also been the vehicle for me to share all that I know with the world.

One of the greatest joys of being a successful writer is the opportunity it briefly creates to touch and enhance the lives of others. It is a tremendously exhilarating and also a deeply humbling experience. Thus to all of you who have been following my books, I hope Feng Shui has indeed brought great good fortune into your lives. Remember that it is not necessary to try to follow every single tip, sentence, or formula given. You must exercise some choices and apply Feng Shui in a clever and creative way. In the process you should enjoy becoming more and more aware of your surroundings. The living earth around us is filled with energy forces that we do not yet understand – some friendly and embracing and others hostile and damaging. Learn to feel the difference by tuning in to these energies. Dissolve all energies that are damaging and make an attempt to harmonize with those energies that bring good fortune. In this way you will really begin to reap the huge rewards that earth luck brings you.

Good luck! And have fun.

LILLIAN TOO

Further Reading

OTHER LILLIAN TOO BOOKS

Basic Feng Shui, KONSEP BOOKS, 1997

Chinese Astrology for Romance and Relationships,
  KONSEP BOOKS, 1996

The Complete Illustrated Guide to Feng Shui, ELEMENT
  BOOKS, 1996

The Complete Illustrated Guide to Feng Shui for Gardens,
  ELEMENT BOOKS, 1998

Creating Abundance with Feng Shui, RIDER, 1999

Easy to Use Feng Shui, COLLINS & BROWN, 1999

Feng Shui, KONSEP BOOKS, 1993

Feng Shui Essentials, RIDER, 1997

Feng Shui Fundamentals: Careers

  Feng Shui Fundamentals: Children

  Feng Shui Fundamentals: Education

  Feng Shui Fundamentals: Eight Easy Lessons

  Feng Shui Fundamentals: Fame

  Feng Shui Fundamentals: Health

  Feng Shui Fundamentals: Love

  Feng Shui Fundamentals: Networking

  Feng Shui Fundamentals: Wealth

ELEMENT BOOKS, 1997

Flying Star Feng Shui, KONSEP BOOKS, 1994
  revised *1999*

The Illustrated Encyclopedia of Feng Shui, ELEMENT BOOKS,
  1999

Lillian Too's Feng Shui Kit, ELEMENT BOOKS,
  1997

The Little Book of Feng Shui, ELEMENT BOOKS,
  1998

The Little Book of Feng Shui at Work, ELEMENT BOOKS,
  1999

Practical Applications of Feng Shui, KONSEP BOOKS,
  1994

Water Feng Shui for Wealth, KONSEP BOOKS,
  1995

LILLIAN TOO'S WEBSITES

You are invited to visit the world's first completely online
Feng Shui magazine at:

http://www.worldoffengshui.com

Lillian Too's official author website where you can check
out all of her 29 Feng Shui books and browse through
Lillian's photo album, read her press cuttings, enjoy her
Feng Shui tips and check out her program of talks and
seminars:

http://www.lillian-too.com

Lillian Too's **Feng Shui Fine Jewelry** site where you
can browse and shop online. OE Design created the
beautiful pieces of real gold and diamond jewelry to
Lillian's specifications. Every piece is designed to activate
a specific type of luck (wealth, romance, career...) for the
wearer using powerful symbolic Feng Shui enhancement:

http://www.lilliantoojewellery.com

Index

Index

Acknowledgments

The publishers wish to thank the following for the use of properties:

Bright Ideas, Lewes

The Last Post, The Barn Collectors Market, Seaford

Heavenly Realms, Eastbourne

Battle Orders, Willingdon

Suttons, Hove

The publishers wish to thank the following for the use of pictures:

Goh Seng Chong 95TC

The Bruce Coleman Collection 55

Corbis Images 10, 84

Liz Eddison 53T, 85, 116, 126

ET *Archive 11*

The Garden Picture Library 74

The Image Bank 40, 67, 80, 132

The Stock Market 19, 35, 51T, 60, 68, 87, 90, 131

Tony Stone Images 8, 15, 34, 42, 54, 82, 86, 93, 94, 104, 112L, 112R, 119

Elizabeth Whiting Associates 66, 110